Into the Blue

Claire Hall

Published by Claire Hall, 2025.

While every precaution has been taken in the preparation of this book, the publisher assumes no responsibility for errors or omissions, or for damages resulting from the use of the information contained herein.

INTO THE BLUE

First edition. April 1, 2025.

Copyright © 2025 Claire Hall.

ISBN: 978-1068308345

Written by Claire Hall.

Table of Contents

Chapter one | The beginning of the end 1
Chapter two | The funeral 14
Chapter Three | The doctors surgery and section 29
Chapter four | New home 40
Chapter five | Therapy plans and wedding plans 57
Chapter six | Prayer mats and a new admission 81
Chapter seven | Breakfast and home leave 95
Chapter eight | Home 115
Chapter nine | Me, bipolar and Irene 136

I dedicate this book to my beautiful son Blue and I hope that it gives light and hope to whomever reads it, like he did to so many in his short life. You will forever be the piece of my heart that's missing until I'm with you again. Love you forever and back Goodnight and God bless.

Chapter one
The beginning of the end

Saturday the 18th of May 2019 was the day that would end up unlocking answers about my

life but also bring me a loss of such magnitude that my life would never be the same again.

Previously I'd only seen on TV or in movies where a single catastrophic event can occur and

within that split second everything irredeemably changes. Despite all of life's ups and downs,

even with all the bad times rolled into one, nothing can ever prepare you for an event like the

one I had to face. It is inconceivable that one's mind can cope with the enormity of a situation

like that.

So here we go.

I stepped out of my front door that Saturday morning with Robert to discover a policeman looking lost. I asked what address he was looking for, to which he replied 22. I told him that that was me, my address, and he asked if we could go inside. Then my worst nightmare unfolded. He said that Blue, my son, had been found unresponsive that morning.

He was sitting on my settee, and I was standing next to the window in my living room. I will never forget the scene as long as I live. Some sort of wail came out of me, and I totally lost the use of my legs. They just gave way and then I was on the floor. Robert just fled the room. Somehow, I regained enough composure to get this done so I could see my son wherever he was. The lovely police officer, doing the absolutely worst part of his job, said he had some formalities but could come back later, to which I said with respect, "I don't want you to come back, I will just get it over with now!" I was desperate to see Blue, he was mine, I didn't want anyone handling him now that they could not save him. He tried to reassure me that he was being taken via ambulance and would very shortly be at the mortuary at the hospital where I have worked for nearly two decades. I just wanted him to go, the rest was really just a blur. All I could think of was that I needed my son, I needed to hold him, I needed to comfort him, I needed to touch his skin, his hair, make him ok. Those thoughts flooded my mind, my being, the entirety of my very soul. My baby, I needed to mend this for him and make him safe and well. Those thoughts not only took my very breath away but also made my heart instantly start to break.

The police officer left. Robert was on the phone and then he came into the living room and just held me. I had lost the power of speech, I was in complete shock. Robert rang the mortuary, but they informed him Blue had just arrived and could we give them an hour or so? How can this be? Making a call like it's just an everyday event! Then Robert said in the gentlest way that we needed to go to my dad's because he was being told. I cried and begged Robert not to make me do it, even the very thought of it was too much for me. My dad had been the dad Blue never had and he was still grieving my other. Robert stood firm and tried to rein in my

INTO THE BLUE

terrible emotional state. I cried and cried but eventually my body followed Robert robotically down to my dad's place three houses down. With every step I took I remember the terrible dread and feelings of doom.

Walking into the house, the house where I lived with my parents and Blue as a baby, was one of

the hardest things I've ever had to do in my life. My sister was there, her husband and other

family members, I cannot remember who. As I walked over to my dad sitting in his chair he was

sobbing and saying why did this have to happen to me, this heartache no parent should ever have to endure. I just knelt at his knees and took his hands. I had no words. His broken heart on top of mine was like I had entered an altogether different type of hell and there was no way back. I still to this day will never know how people can endure that sort of heartache and not die of a broken heart. The term heartache is sometimes loosely used, but if you have ever had to experience real heartache you will know that you can literally feel your heart aching and it feels like eventually it will give up and die. Your own torment and torture were more than enough, never mind witnessing your loved ones going through it too. The distress and pain are indescribable and there is no cure other than time.

I was desperate to see Blue. The need was so intense and urgent, it is inexpressible and impossible to explain. I can't remember getting to the mortuary, I just remember myself, Robert, my dad and the rest of the family being met by Karen the mortuary manager, who I knew, in the waiting area. She informed us that they had taken great care of Blue and that he was ready for us in the next room. Robert reacted first and said through tears that he was so sorry, but he could not come in with me. I looked around the room and came to Dawn, my niece, who is steady as a rock and was training to be a nurse, so straight away I asked her to come in with me. I needed someone with the best possible potential of not breaking down. As we came around the curtain that we were met with after entering the room, there was Blue, my child, my flesh and blood, lying on a raised platform with a velvet blanket neatly over him up to his chest. Seeing his still body and tainted skin, and touching his cold limbs, made my mind go numb and then suddenly fill with racing thoughts of fear and denial. I kissed his face and held his hand, not fully comprehending the situation. I didn't really know then that shock was taking over.

I asked Dawn to take a photo of his chest, all while pulling up his neat and immaculately clean tracksuit top in a state of panic. She asked me why. I said with desperation that I wanted photos of the tattoos on his chest before a post-mortem happened. She did exactly as I asked. I noticed one of his sleeves had been cut above the elbow and realised this was for IV access, but a closer look at his arm showed no attempt had been made, which gave me some idea of his status when they got to him. Which then made my mind go to an altogether different place, wondering how long he had been dead. Why did no one who was with him do anything? Why did this ever need to happen? I work in ITU, and we sadly get lots of young people who have overdosed, and

INTO THE BLUE

the doctors put them on a ventilator, give them fluids to keep their blood pressure and drugs to regulate their hearts. The very next day in most cases they come off the ventilator and are good to go to the ward or home. Why, when they noticed he was becoming unconscious, did they not get help? They wouldn't have got in any trouble and my beautiful son would still be here. All of this could have been prevented, his death and probably so many others.

We came out and then little by little everyone went in to see him. I don't know the order, or even who went in with my dad, I think I didn't have room left for any more hurt. I went in again before leaving, with Robert this time, and it was totally unthinkable. It wasn't just seeing him, it was leaving him that was so unbearably hard. I was touching him, feeling his hair, looking at him but not really believing the situation. I think the magnitude is far too great for your mind to comprehend.

I can't remember leaving or getting back to the house. That night or day or whatever time it was, friends and neighbours came. During that time Robert came in and asked if he could speak to me in the other room for a minute. Not sure what was going on now, I just went in. He told me he had just taken a phone call from Blue's dad's friend and asked me to just listen to him before giving an answer. I then guessed, I'm not sure why, what he was about to say. He said that this friend rang to say George was distraught about Blue when he found out and he knew it was a big ask but could George go and see Blue at the mortuary. Without hesitation I said yes, the most horrific thing had just happened, and nothing could ever be harder than the hell I was living. I felt deep in my heart that I needed God to take great care of my child and I needed to start this journey in a way of forgiveness and love, no matter what water had gone under the bridge.

All I remember after that is later being in my bed with Emma and Val, my friends, lying over me with 'I love Tom Hardy' eye masks on, pouring drinks into my mouth, joking, talking and talking. I think they were just trying their hardest to fill in the gaps, but what they didn't realise was, it was a humongous crater of hell on earth that couldn't be filled, though to be fair, even I didn't realise the extent of it at the time. I slept with the help of copious amounts of alcohol and zopiclone, which the GP had administered unawares to me. When I woke in the morning, I just let out an animalistic cry, a cry no one ever should experience, from the deepest part of my soul. I had had only one big loss before Blue and that was when my mam died. I suffered horrendous sorrow, and it ended up making me very ill. I loved her more than life itself, but it is nothing like the loss of a child – that is truly a part of your soul, your very being, a piece of your heart. The only thing I remember that day was lots of flowers arriving – his gym sent lovely flowers, they were some of the first to arrive – and then arranging to go up to the mortuary again so George could see Blue. All I remember was that it was dark when we arrived. Val had come with us and when Robert parked the car, I told him not to ask me to go in and that this was enough. Val got out with Robert to greet George; his friend was also with him. Robert being Robert came back to the car and said this was the last thing he would ask of me, would I get out of the car and come in and sit in the waiting area for when George came out from seeing Blue? He said he truly thought it was the right thing to do. I had little concentration at that time, never mind judgement, I just got out of the car and walked into the waiting area, numb to the whole situation. I think your brain is clever and the shock creates some of that numbness.

George came out of the room after seeing Blue and just fell at my feet, crying and begging for forgiveness. He hadn't been a parent to Blue since he was five years old; I wasn't even sure if he had seen him as an adult. His pain and regret were real, so I told him that Blue's death was enough. This was enough. I knew that I was instantly going to forgive and forget somehow. I knew that this was all I had room for, and I did in my heart do all of the above. Call it divine intervention I don't know, all I can say is I knew it was the right way to be. I was mentally and emotionally drained and just wanted peace. I went in to see Blue before I left – I can't remember who I was with – then once more went home. This time when I lay down in bed the same noise came out of me. Somehow the darkness of the night caused great pain and the light of the dawn was the same. I remember the gravity of one more night or morning starting without my son was unbearable. Hence every night and morning came the same noise and a feeling that my very soul and heart were being ripped out of me. That went on for well over a year every night and every morning.

I remember that month of May 2019 the weather was glorious, I would just get up and go in the garden and smoke and someone, anyone who was there, would put a tea, whatever, in front of me. The garden was the place I would just sit and sit. Family and friends would come and go, for me when I look back it was comforting but at the time I barely noticed.

Except one particular time, my niece's daughter Freya came, she obviously had been told about Blue's death and was hell-bent on cheering me up! She asked me to be Simon Cowell and judge her audition. It was all above board, I had to sit facing the raised decking area while she positioned herself in between the two posts. I pressed play on my iPhone and Lady Gaga's 'Bad Romance' blasted from the speaker at her request. What my eyes witnessed can only be described as the most X-rated performance that not even an adult should do, or Lady Gaga for that matter, never mind a six-year-old. I laughed that hard I wet myself. I didn't think that was possible, so thank you, Freya, for that memorable moment.

I had an overwhelming feeling that Blue would want to look his best when it came to his funeral. And I wanted him home the night before, I knew that for definite, it's an old-fashioned thing and I really regretted not doing that for my

INTO THE BLUE

mam. I couldn't get up to the mortuary quick enough with an idea in mind. I spoke with Karen, the senior technician who I knew. I explained the situation and told her I was going to have Watsons funeral directors, which my family always used. I asked what was better: the fridge in the mortuary or the undertaker's to keep Blue looking his very best? This may seem unnervingly clinical and strange to many people, but maybe it was all my years working in ITU that kicked in, or the shock, which absolutely makes you a different person. Karen understood, thank the Lord. She asked me to wait while she went to ask Michael, because he used to embalm and knew everything there was to know about the preservation side. When she came back, she informed me that the fridge was way better than a cold room at the undertaker's. She then told me that they had enough room and could keep Blue there for me, also stating for the same reason it was better that Blue did not come in and out of the fridge for more viewings etc if that's what I wanted. That gave me some sort of peace, oddly enough. I'm not sure why; maybe it's because all you have left is those last acts that you can do for your loved one. I had one more favour to ask of her: I wanted to bathe Blue, I had to! I had laid out so many people, too many to remember on ITU, all of them someone's loved one but all a stranger to me. I needed this last request more than life itself.

Karen did as she promised and got back to me. They agreed I could wash him. Karen explained that their setting couldn't be more removed from a bed space on ITU, and went on to say the room we would have to use was very clinical and was the actual room they used to wash the bodies after their post-mortem had been done. I said that was ok. I was that desperate to be able to do this last thing for my son I would have done it in a field, anywhere as long as I could do it.

Straight off the phone I ran upstairs, got out my fluffiest white towel and face cloth, the lovely Elemis products he loved so much that they were nearly finished, and my beautiful Givenchy shopper to put them all in. I knew that when I brought them back home, I would keep them forever, never to get out again! So that last smell, that last wash was on them forever! When Dawn called in, I asked her if she would come with me. I knew in my heart that I would do it no matter how terrible it was, but I just needed moral support, and she agreed.

That walk to the hospital, which was about ten to fifteen minutes from my house, was like walking towards doomsday. I knew this was the last thing I would ever do for him, bar having him home the night before the funeral, but then the undertakers would have dressed him etc. The undertakers informed me when I told them that he was staying at the mortuary that they would need to get him from the hospital mortuary for a few hours before they brought him home and that they would need his clothes and anything else he would be wearing.

I remember there was not much said on the walk there. What do you say to each other? I think there was a bit of small talk, but probably both our minds were full of trepidation and sadness about what was about to occur. It helped that we both worked at the hospital, for the small part, as we had both delivered last offices before, although we both knew without saying anything to each other that that's where the similarities ended.

INTO THE BLUE

When we arrived at the hospital mortuary Karen was there to greet us. When I asked if Dawn could come in with me, she informed me that I had to go in alone as even that was pushing everyone's luck. This had never been done before and I hadn't even realised until that point this was sort of being done on the QT. Secretly though I thought he's my son, and if I want to wash him that is my God given right and no one or anything would have stopped me from doing so.

As I followed Karen into the room where Blue was, I was blinded by the bright lights bouncing off the gleaming white walls. There was nothing on the right side of the room and on the left was what can only be described as a long steel trough midway up the wall with shower heads connected. There on the right of the trough was a trolley pushed into it and on that trolley was my son's lifeless body. He had an NHS towel over his middle and his head was supported by a block underneath it. I tried hard to hide my darkest distraught feelings and the wobbling going on in my legs, all the while trying to talk myself down from losing it completely. I needed to do this. I had to try and have some composure, any amount would do.

As I walked towards him, bag in hand, I was slowly starting to grasp the enormity and the great sadness about what was about to happen.

The lovely Michael, the other mortuary technician, was quietly busying himself at the side. I plucked up the courage to start getting things out of my bag, sort of readying myself and giving them the ok that we could start. Michael was great. He just went with it and acted perfectly normal, as normal as he could be in this situation. Like we had a job to get done, which was exactly how I needed him to be.

I didn't know where to start. I was looking at his body, his face, and I literally didn't know what to do. Poor Michael must have gathered this, and he just started washing Blue's lower limbs. Bearing in mind Blue had already been washed and this was just for me, I got out the face cloth and tried to jolly things along by saying out loud that the Elemis face wash, that I hadn't even used, was almost gone as Blue loved it so much, as if that would do it.

I started to wash his face and Michael informed me as kindly as possible not to move the back of his head or move the towel from his abdomen due to his post-mortem. The words just seemed to get jumbled up in my head with all the other thoughts – that this wasn't real, and I would soon wake up. The water was absolutely freezing. In fact, everything from the cold water, the stainless steel, the clinical room, the block under his head, the towel over his middle was the opposite of what I was used to, and this was my son!!! How did this happen? Why was I here? Why was I doing this? Let me know this is just a nightmare and that none of it is real.

As I moved down his arm – it was a robotic action by this time – I was hovering towards a point of shock when Michael broke into my thoughts. He asked did I have photos of all Blue's tattoos? I wasn't sure, so he offered to take photos of them all. I agreed and gave him my phone. I told Michael that I always cut Blue's toenails and that the standing joke was that even though I used baby scissors he jump before I even got near them. He then asked me if I had them with me, to which I replied no. He said he could get his nail clippers out of his locker and clip them if I wanted, and that he would also get a specimen pot and put them in so I could keep them. When he came back, I was still in the same spot. I could barely move, it was taking everything in me to not lose it.

After finishing with Blue's feet, Michael asked me if I had a song I would like to play, as they had an amazing speaker that they used when it was out of hours and no one was around. I got it; when you do things on a daily basis like this you need these small things to get by. The words just came out of my mouth! I said I had a song picked out for his funeral, it was 'Leave a Light On' by Tom Walker and the Red Hot Chilli Pipers. He asked should he put it on, to which I said yes.

Blasting out of the speakers was this magnificent song, unbelievably sad but so ethereal, and I lost it. I clenched Blue with both my hands and my head fell onto his arm. I could hardly get my breath as the majestic bagpipes played in the background.

For all that was one of the hardest things I've ever done in my life I wouldn't take it back, not for a minute, or change a single thing. I'm pleased I did that for my son and that I have the memory of it. Then the time came again when I had to leave him there, and this time was for the last time. I am forever grateful for being able to bathe him and for him being able to stay there. So, when it came to him coming home before his funeral, he looked his best, the way he would have wanted it.

On the walk home myself and Dawn talked about what happened like we would talk about a handover at work. I think it's the only way we could, looking back.

7

Chapter two
The funeral

Next the funeral arrangements had to be made. This is going to be very much other people's story, i.e. family members as I didn't, or should I say couldn't, participate for the most part as I was now becoming seriously unwell. All I remember was again sitting in the garden, beautiful sunshine, smoking and smoking, and my family members coming and going. We agreed that my sister, sister-in-law, and niece would go to the florist's, all I asked for was that my flowers be white and baby blue. I did not know anything about who was going to conduct the funeral, nor did I ask, I was, unbeknownst to me, withdrawing into a world of my own. I remember watching a documentary film called *Free Solo*. I was so engrossed by the amazing feat and unbelievable courage it took for this man to scale El Capitan, the mecca of all cliff faces in Yosemite Park, with not a single rope! It had never been achieved before and the risk of falling to his death was in every single second of his climb, every slight move of a foot, hand or finger. I had the volume on full blast! I didn't realise at the time, I just thought I couldn't hear it, but my concentration skills weren't working. I had a little shrine, if you will, by the TV cabinet, cards, flowers, candles etc, and on a piece of paper I wrote *My free solo*. Blue in his little life in my eyes had been that, taking risks and eventually he took the wrong one and now here we all were.

INTO THE BLUE

At some point – not sure when it happened but it was obviously before I washed Blue – I was lying in bed, it was nighttime, Robert was lying next to me, and he asked if I had thought about songs for the funeral. Straight away I said I wanted Queen, 'Who Wants To Live Forever' for going in and then 'Leave a Light On' by Tom Walker. It's mad how even when your mind is that full, you're not even able to process things, but then the senses kick in when you're reminded of the importance of certain things. Robert googled 'Leave a Light On' and came across the Chilli Pipers' version. He then went on to play it full volume in the darkness. I remember being mesmerised by it, the bagpipes, his voice, the message it relayed, in fact everything about it. That was it, the song that would be played while everyone stood in silence for Blue, before being seated.

It came to my mind that I needed something to wear for the funeral ASAP. I told Robert I needed to go to Fenwick's the next day, and he asked what I was thinking of. I told him that I wanted to be as smart as I could, I wanted to make my son proud for his send-off. Robert asked where in Fenwick's and I said probably only Hugo Boss would do! I've always been this way with clothes, things, any kind of shopping, but when I'm fast it's on another level. Poor Robert just went with it, he just wanted more than anything else in the world to make this horrific situation slightly easier. At that time though I just needed it to be quick and done so it was sorted and over with as soon as possible.

So, in Fenwick's we went straight to the Boss concession. I needed no direction, I know the shop like the back of my hand. We must have looked so dishevelled, luckily there was an older woman on that day. I think Robert had a quiet word with her informing her what the clothes were for. She was of Libyan descent, I think, and had this unbelievable calmness about her that I'll never forget.

I remember she was so serene and gentle, picking clothing and accessories etc, i.e. shoes and bags and placing them in the changing room, so I could just go in and try them on rather than looking through the numerous rails. The suit I chose didn't really have a suitable blouse or shirt to go underneath it, so she went to another concession and came back with lots of options.

There I had it, a suit, a blouse, and shoes. I didn't need a bag as I had a Boss one at home that went perfectly, a Christmas present from Robert. While she packed the items so beautifully, Robert and I sat in a heap on a small chair-sofa thoroughly exhausted from the whole experience.

Then they were hung up in my dressing room, all set out, shoes, bag, everything, like I was going to a wedding or something! These things were just done on some sort of autopilot. I know that is hard to understand, but it's true.

As the time grew nearer, it was a dread like I'd never felt before nor probably ever will again! The finality was unthinkable. All I could do was robotically go along with it. As they say, time waits for no man.

Blue had come home as arranged to my mam and dad's house as I had wanted. My mind shut it out. I knew the funeral was the next day, but I totally blocked out the fact that he was now home. It may have been a coping method or something that had kicked in. I don't know why, or how, it happened, but it would end up being one of my biggest regrets!

INTO THE BLUE

Unbeknown to me my nieces and sister and father had made the living room beautiful with candles, twinkle lights, but very cold, bless them, to keep Blue the way he was.

He was dressed in a white shirt and black trousers, and even down to his socks and underwear everything was the best. The undertakers had dressed him while they had him for a few hours, to do whatever they do. Danielle, my niece, had only needed to use a little bit of gel on his hair, and told me later that she had to put a small amount of make-up on one of his ears that was slightly discoloured. But other than that he looked beautiful. He would have been happy with how he looked, I wanted that for him above anything else.

His friends arrived at different times to see him and say their goodbyes. I'm pleased that everyone had that time with him and that it was not at an undertaker's, it was in his and my home. We had lived there when Blue was born, and it continued to be a place we returned throughout our lives. Also, my lovely dad was so proud when I asked him if Blue could come home. He loved him like I did. How he did it all I don't know, he was still grieving my mam and missed her the same way as he had from the day she died.

Like I said before, looking back I have to live with the regret of not spending that time with Blue for as long as I live, even though I could not really be responsible at the time, my head was not well. However, it fills me with great peace that my family and Blue's friends had that time, it was more important than we all realised.

My mind had continued to disregard the fact that Blue was now home. Robert even made me go out with the dog on the nighttime, the eve of his funeral, on the way back directing us so that we had to pass my parents' house. It still didn't resonate with me at all, I just walked past the door like it was somehow normal. I don't understand it entirely myself. Robert said later he wanted me to choose with my feet, not wanting to rock the already unsteady boat. He knew then that I wasn't well. Sadly no one reminded me or asked me to go and see him or even tell me he was home. I don't blame anyone, it was an awful predicament.

The morning of the funeral I woke up with the same animal-sounding wail, then at whatever point just proceeded to get ready. I remember when I was getting dressed Robert gave me a present. It consisted of a beautiful necklace with a blue heart on, a bracelet with two blue hearts (appropriately), a lovely black Boss bag, and shoes to match. He had already bought me a stunning pair of cream shoes from Boss when he bought my suit etc, but insisted I wear the black ones for the crematorium and then change them for the afterwards. I just followed instructions that morning, not really knowing what to do myself. My mind was full and blank at the same time.

When the time came, I stepped out of my house. My neighbour, Blue's friend, was there, and Val, my childhood friend, was walking down towards us. As we were nearing my dad's house, I can remember my brother came out. I hadn't realised until I saw Bri wearing a blue shirt that Robert had a blue shirt on too.

I floated into my dad's house. All the people, family, were just a haze, but somehow my legs took me over to Blue in his coffin, all white and glossy. My child! He really was just lying there, still, motionless, although so handsome, how can this be? He is so beautiful, loving and kind! He cannot be in a coffin with funeral cars at the bottom of the street waiting for him! I'm not really going to my child's funeral, stop this, rewind, take it all back, reverse time I'm begging you, God!

Then a voice woke me from my own mind. It was time to leave, the undertaker was telling us. I must have just followed suit from then on in.

I remember the beautiful cross, so innocent-looking, the most stunning baby-blue flowers sitting in the middle of a sea of white flowers, which was placed on the top of his coffin. The car journey with everyone trying to stifle their tears as I had not shed one yet. I could hear the snuffles going on but never turned to look. Then we were at the crematorium. Later Robert told me that the people spilled all the way down to the main road. He had never seen that many people before at someone's funeral, Blue would have loved that.

George was the first person I saw as I got out of the car. He was standing to one side as he was one of the pallbearers carrying the coffin, which had been arranged prior. I had forgotten that I suggested that too. We walked in as 'Who Wants To Live Forever' played. I still love how the beginning is so theatrical and haunting. Music has always played a huge part in my life, but never more so than now. I had asked for Daniel, my nephew, to be seated to my right as he had a real calming influence, and Robert to my left, then my dad on his left. I knew I wouldn't have the strength to sit next to my father. Everyone else sort of had each other.

We were standing before Blue when 'Leave A Light On' played, and it was how I imagined – so ethereal, but also with a message that I thought was so important to get across to anyone there who needed to hear it. You see, it doesn't matter to me how my son died. Yes it was drugs, but if you had the terrible misfortune to lose a child you would understand that, afterwards, it really isn't the how.

We then sat as the service proceeded, which I had no part in. My family had chosen wisely, I don't think I could have coped. They had the lovely humanist Val, who also conducted my mother's service, and the place was full to the rafters, in fact the people standing could not even move an inch. Halfway through my two nieces, Dawn and Lynsey, got up and read a eulogy they had written. To my horror later I was told I chatted all the way through, recalling and agreeing with things that were said while smoking my fake tab. Daniel tried to rein me in, but to be fair he was up against it. This was the start of my spiral.

INTO THE BLUE

At the end of the service Blue's friend Sharna came from the back of the crowd with a mic in her hand. Blue had in the past spent endless hours trying to boost her confidence, i.e. getting her to sing in front of him at every opportunity and telling her how good she was, she now has music produced, He knows she knows! Is the name on her label. Now she and her partner sang 'It's Been a Long Day' by Charlie Puth. It was amazing how strong she must have been to have done that. Her partner did the rap vocals, and I think everyone must have been as stunned as I was. Much later my old neighbour Bob, who never shied away from speaking his mind, and had also lost a son, said it was the most beautiful funeral he had ever attended.

Then it was the wake. We held it at a local social club so we could fit everyone in. I remember being in the loo with Val and numerous others, having a meltdown! The same Givenchy bag I used when bathing Blue, which I had prepared the night before with careful precision, somehow didn't have the white T-shirt in it that I wanted. Jess, Blue's friend, and Lynsey my niece were frantically looking inside it to no avail. I was standing in my bra half dressed, pint at the ready and smoking a tab out the window. The real reason, I think now, was that I just didn't want to go into a room full of people with that certain look on their faces, wondering what they could say. Literally Heaven-sent, at the bottom of the bag was Blue's primary school T-shirt that he hand-painted then printed himself at Kells Lane Primary school, for their centenary year. I can't ever remember putting it in. I pulled it on, although it was small, and loved the fact that I was now wearing that.

So, armed with wearing Blue's beautiful T-shirt, I changed my shoes from black to cream. Jess was taking my bag home

ASAP – the same habits I've had all my life never left, even for this. I walked straight down to the bottom of the room, never looking at anyone for more than a split second, not giving them time to ask any questions or give me that look I was quickly starting to recognise, then out to the smoking area.

I spotted my friends from work and thought they were a safe bet, after all they were ITU nurses, used to death, used to grieving families and parents. I was right, they were much less awkward, and greeted me the same as always. I'm not knocking people – don't get me wrong, I've been exactly the same in their situations – but that day was hard enough and this bit I just wanted to sail through it somehow. So, there I was chatting with Gary and Spires thinking I was being perfectly normal, when in fact I was like an excitable child, my other half was in full flow. The other half that I had no name for yet. I informed Gary that I wanted him to marry Fiaz, our other friend, and that he wasn't thinking straight if he didn't think it was a good idea. Then I reeled off all the reasons why it was the best idea all round. Somehow Gary and Spires managed to pull off a madcap conversation in style. To be fair, it is my personality just on steroids, and we were at my son's funeral.

Then I remember looking up in awe as Cheryl, my cousin's daughter, came walking over to us. She was carrying a tray of shots. What I was in awe of was the blue blouse she was wearing, the way it was flowing around in the wind almost like a cloud. I have a vivid memory even now of how absolutely beautiful it looked, how angelic. In my head I was the only one seeing and thinking this, but then again this wasn't new to me either, these intense thoughts and feelings, they were part of me, coming and going for as long as I can remember.

INTO THE BLUE

The rest of that day was a bit of a blur, like my mother's wake. I just wandered around and around the room aimlessly. At some point Emma and Val asked me if I wanted to go to another pub as everyone was leaving, and I blindly got in the taxi when it came, it was just an action. Then I was in the Big Market in Newcastle, and we went to the first pub where music was on. It's mad how your mind is really switched off and literally you simply do things, there is no thought process that leads you there. We did shots at the bar. I think you could have given me gallons that day and it wouldn't have even made a dent. I do remember Emma and Val doing forward rolls across the dance floor, and their attempts to make me laugh or join in, but it was never going to work. I went outside for a tab, and some Dutch bloke – I think he was Dutch – tried to chat me up. I told him to piss off, which he did, and I finished my tab in peace.

One of them took a phone call and then we were off in another taxi, this time landing at my niece Danielle's house. She lives just up the street from me. Friends, neighbours and family had gone back to Danielle's, bringing the buffet back with them together with a load of booze. I'm not sure how long I was there, but not long, I think. My lovely neighbours Norma and Steve walked me home. Once the door was locked, I proceeded to climb the stairs. I hung my suit up, washed my make-up off, cleaned my teeth and got into bed. All the in-betweens I don't remember, but old habits, especially with me, defo die hard.

The next few weeks were all a bit mad. The following is my recollection. I had begun to lose the plot so excuse the order of events. I'll try my best to keep them right. I had no idea of times, dates etc, I barely knew if it was day or night!

That following week, I asked Robert to take me to the shops at the industrial park at the Team Valley. I needed to go to the pound shop, it's anybody's guess why. He waited in the car; I think he was mentally spent by then or not far off. It was wondrous to me – as soon as I walked in, shelves upon shelves of stuff. I started picking things off the shelves like it was *Supermarket Sweep*! Then it dawned on me that I needed a basket. A trolley would have been better, but they didn't have them. Aw, the book area – you name it, children's books, teenage books, every type got put in the basket just because I liked the cover. Then I spotted the flip flops. They were a good idea for the summer holiday that was never going to get booked. Babygros, I needed them. They were so cute and for some reason they were giving me comfort putting them in my basket, which was now overflowing. It was ok, I could carry stuff in my other hand. A couple in the next aisle were staring, probably at the sheer excessiveness of it all, but it went straight over my head!

All the stationery I could carry, all the funky things I could see, a bit like finding treasure, I was over the moon with my finds. On making my way to the till, only because I couldn't carry anything else, I saw my brother at the entrance of the shop, his face registering something between astonishment and fear. I thought instantly that he had come to stop me, so I shouted something along the lines of 'don't come over'. He didn't, to my surprise, and looking back I think he was too afraid to. When someone is mentally unwell most people, unless they are trained, just don't know what to do, wary of making the situation worse than it already is. Over a hundred pounds later I walked out of the shop with the funkiest carrier bags ever, laden with all my goods. My brother and brother-in-law were standing in the car park. I just walked past them to the boot of the car, like it was all normal, I had just been shopping that was all. Robert, sick of his life I think, just closed the boot and off home we went. I've still got some of the things, as a bit of a reminder. The Babygros my family took, I think maybe they thought that was just too sad.

The next escapade was in Newcastle. Not sure what my excuse for that was, but poor Robert had to take me again. While walking in the Monument area I spotted Scribbler, you can probably guess, another stationery shop, my childhood favourite. Robert refused to go in, and I don't blame him. I had no idea about any sort of cash flow in my bank, it didn't matter because I never gave it more than a second's thought. Straight to the Trump doll – hilarious, I'm definitely having that – then on to pens, pencils, coasters. Too many to choose, I'll take one of each. At the till the young guy serving me asked if I always shopped like this, to which I said "Pretty much, yeah." Robert looked furious when I came out of the shop, which in turn made me mad, he was spoiling my day. Then I had a thought – we could go to Harry's bar for a drink, that would make it better. Robert refused but I just walked on regardless. He followed me of course, but while doing so he rang my siblings to get over and help deal with me again. I walked into the bar. Robert did not follow and, not even remembering that I had my bank card, the one that I had just used, I walked out thinking that I had no money to buy a drink. I went onto the little terrace area where an elderly woman was sitting on her own. Thinking it was meant to be, different company, I plonked myself next to her. It looked to me like she was lonely, so I proceeded to chat to her as if I had known her all my life. No clue what I spoke about. The next minute my brother, sister and sister-in-law landed, and they coaxed me into the car by saying they were having a drink at my sister's house. I think they must have just thought if it's a drink she wants it's best to be somewhere safe.

As we neared my sister's house, I made them stop at the shop on the estate. I went in and bought numerous bottles of shots, to the shopkeeper's glee. Then at my sister's house I thought 'right let's get started', shot glasses out on the bench and started pouring. Apparently at a certain point my sister and sister-in-law thought I had hollow legs. They were starting to feel quite intoxicated, and they said I looked like I hadn't even had a drink. I think certain parts of my brain at that time were switched off – not very helpful! Next minute I needed to nip to my house. I think I lied about the reason, the paranoia kicks in and you must listen to it cause after all that's the truth, and nothing else is. Like I've said before, I love to shop, so the real reason I wanted to go to my house was to change. I must be going out if I'm drinking, even if they weren't coming with me. Up in my dressing room, amongst the couple of hundred pairs of shoes – no that's not an exaggeration – I found the most stunning pair. I had forgotten I had them. They were transparent, like Cinderella's slippers but better! So, I put them on and changed my top, thinking that will do, the shoes are enough on their own! When I arrived back at my sister's house, to my shock my sister looked spent, and my sister-in-law was making excuses about needing to go home. I know, I thought, I would just go out by myself, so out the door I went and started to run, no idea where I was going. I just felt the fight or flight feeling overwhelm my whole being. Running across the park path, all in my four-and-whatever-inch shoes. My brother and brother-in-law were running after me, it was like cat and mouse. I remember thinking at that time this is a game! I got to the end of the park path and then couldn't figure out where or how to go anywhere next. My brain wasn't even capable of getting me further than the end of my estate.

The next few days I didn't apparently venture anywhere, but it was too late then, no one trusted me or was willing to leave me by myself at that point. Robert asked some of my friends from work who were experienced ITU nurses to come and have a look at me, maybe to make the same assessment as him but in concrete. They came and soon realised I did need medical attention.

CLAIRE HALL

Chapter Three
The doctors surgery and section

The doctor's surgery. I'm in a full-to-capacity waiting room with Robert, brother and sister in tow. I was pissed that I was there, for one thing, then the songs being played on the overhead radio were just sending me over the edge. They were doing it on purpose. The surgery knew if they played enough sentimental tunes that they would get me to behave the way they wanted me to. I wasn't going to play that game. I was pacing up and down trying to keep my temper in check. Then bingo! Johnny Mathis's, 'When a Child Is Born' came on, one of my dad's favourite songs. My child was dead, what were they doing to me? That's when the Tourette's started, the swearing, losing control at an exponential rate. An elderly gentleman sitting with a seat between himself and Robert brought me literally back into the room. He gently suggested that I sit down next to him and stop the swearing as it wasn't the way I really wanted to be. I did as he said and sat down next to him, not daring to say that the surgery was deliberately playing these songs and that they were the ones at fault. I didn't trust anyone at this point.

Dr Ward came out and called me in. I think even the receptionists realised how poorly I was by then and may have informed him. Once in his room, I can't remember what he said to begin with, but I just proceeded to pace around his room, talking and talking. At some point he was sitting at his desk eating his healthy sandwich while I asked him if he was married etc. Where was his ring? How many children did he have? Why did his children have biblical names? And so on and so on. I certainly don't remember much. Apparently, I was in his office a couple of hours, and he had made the call for a team of doctors to come so I could be sectioned, that's why he was keeping me there. I wanted to go out for a cigarette. My family were worried that I might abscond, but Dr Ward reassured them that I was free, for the minute anyway, and if I did, he would just have to call the police. I had a cigarette with my sister and obligingly went straight back in, because at that time I not only didn't know that I was about to be sectioned, but I was also acting like it was just a trip out at the doctor's. I didn't even know why I was there. I work in ITU, so you can imagine how poorly my mind was, acting like I was at a friend's house, my doctor being the friend.

The team came. I recall an older lady, a younger male and a young female. All I remember is they asked, 'did I think I was well?' to which I said a committed "YES"! Then Bob's your uncle, a white van and two paramedics arrived for me! And no, it isn't an urban myth, it really does happen.

The white van had a lovely carpeted floor with strobe lighting all the way to the back, a bit like a party bus. I thought it was a great idea to have it on the floor. Peculiarly there was a cage built into the back of the bus/van. I had no idea what that was for. I imagined we must be going somewhere now, with myself and Robert on the bus. Yeah, we were, we were going straight to the Tranwell psychiatric hospital. I still never clicked when we got there, even though I knew the building and what it was all about. I have even done some bank shifts there, albeit on the lower floor of the building. So, I should have known exactly what this meant, but I was that poorly I had no clue.

Up the stairs we went, the paramedics buzzed to get us into the secure unit and inside we were greeted by friendly staff. I can remember looking at Robert and thinking how terribly sad he looked.

The next thing, myself and Robert were in a room with chairs and a little coffee table, for whatever reason I still had not understood. Then a very tall man in a suit came in, so I gathered he was important and that I needed to pay attention. This situation looked like it needed that!

Robert told me later that he was the consultant on the unit, Dr Sem, he was Dutch. He had apparently gone on to explain the legality of my section and what it would imply. At some point after that Robert was given the nod so to speak to leave, and he said he could hear me hammering on the locked doors with my fists as he walked along the corridor. Once outside the building he said he just stood with his back against the wall and wept. He thought that was it, I would never be well ever again.

At this point I think just enough of my brain was working to know that I was going to be kept there. I still had my mobile phone, so I went into the toilet and locked the door, sweating, trying to think quickly about my escape plan. I rang ITU first. The nurse in charge answered, who I knew. I asked her to get Fiaz for me. He is an ITU consultant, but he is my friend first and yes, he would be able to get me out of here. To my surprise the nurse informed me that she was sorry but the unit was really busy and Fiaz was also busy in a bedspace. I then suggested any other consultant would do, but she insisted that none of them were free. Not knowing that, obviously they all knew about Blue and when I told her that I was in Tranwell and needed help, it didn't take much for her to put two and two together.

After I got off the phone from her, I rang 999 and asked for the fire brigade. Very quietly, almost in a whisper, I told them that I was a staff member at the psychiatric hospital and a patient had started a fire and I had locked myself in the bathroom to make this call; only the latter was true. Straight after that I rang Glenis my friend who I had worked with at the hospital since I started. She was actually at the entrance of A&E when she answered the phone. I asked her to come for me, apparently, I was begging her to get me out. I then told her that I had to go as the fire brigade were arriving. Glenis heard the sirens passing her while she was on the phone. I know, I thought next, Clare! She lived close, as in five minutes away, she is a well-respected ITU nurse! Yes! she answered, I hurriedly told her my situation and begged her to come. She agreed. I was right then, and they are in the wrong. No way would Clare come unless it was the right thing to do. Now for the fire brigade! They will break the doors in for Clare to get me out, I would be sorted.

I was stood at the entrance doors of the unit which were glass-panelled fire doors as the fire brigade arrived. I could see through the glass the first fireman with axe in hand and Clare stood beside him. That will be imprinted in my memory forever and probably hers too. Staff buzzed them in but lo and behold that never worked either. As soon as they were informed I was actually an inpatient, off they trotted. So I started frantically pulling all the documentation off the walls, which ironically were patients' rights, and tried to stick them all to my top. They were falling off as quickly as I put them on. Plan F, I took my top off, thinking my skin would be more adhesive maybe, at which point Clare told the staff that I was her friend and work colleague, also she was a nurse up at the hospital. She suggested, probably because I was profuse by that point, that maybe if she took me out for a cigarette, I might calm down a little. Yes, you guessed their answer: a resounding no.

They must have had enough by then, as two male staff came from the male wing and took my arms and started marching me down the unit. The male on my left was digging his fingers and nails into my wrist. I told him to get his hands off me, I would walk by myself, which I did. As I neared the bottom there they were, the three doctors who had come to the surgery to see me. I started screaming at them, "My son has died! I'm not fucking mad, I'm grieving!" and brandishing in her face a photo on my phone of my son's dead body. The older women looked really scared, but the younger one nodded her head in agreement, which did make me stop what I was doing. I think her acknowledgement in a way calmed me, her agreeing with me with the tilt of her head was such a small gesture but it worked, momentarily.

I was led into a room. It was all white with an electric blue double-size mattress with a built-in pillow and a chair which was exactly the same colour and material on the floor. Remember the blue gym mats at school? The same as that but more padded. The toilet and sink were to one side, open to the room, and when I turned there was what I can only describe as a box with a window in it facing into the room. Then there was just me, alone. Well, what was I going to do now? My mind was spinning. I couldn't believe it. What, it wasn't enough that my child had died, now they were going to torture me? Well, I wasn't going to give up without a fight, that was for sure!

A person appeared at the window in the box. He had a uniform on, so he was staff. Right, I'll give him a piece of my mind! My temper was off the charts. I started shouting at him, "I'm not the fucking IRA and I won't be here long enough for a hunger strike, but I'm not going to intake any fluids whatsoever. Ha! You will have to take me up to ITU for a cannula to be put in my arm to give me IV fluids and when you do you will all be in fucking trouble!"

He never flinched, and on closer inspection he seemed to be writing something down. What the frig was he writing? They were the ones that were going to send me nuts, never mind anything else. When that didn't work, I was sitting on the mattress frantically thinking about what I could do next when I saw a twenty pence piece on the floor. All my birthdays had come at once! They had obviously missed it, as there was absolutely nothing else on the floor, or anywhere else for that matter. I considered for a time, what to do? With no other ideas really, I held it up in front of the glass and said, "Look at what you forgot! I'm going to swallow it, then I'll choke, and you will all get the blame!" I didn't really fancy putting it in my mouth, but I had run out of options. Here we go, down the hatch. I stretched it out as long as I could, but to my surprise I couldn't even get it down my mouth was so dry. I didn't even realise that I could have just gone over to the sink for water, it never even entered my mind. People think when you're seriously mentally unwell like that, you would have no memory of any of the events during that time, and I would have thought that too. Now I'm proof that you can have quite a bit of insight and knowledge of the time you were unwell, or having a psychotic episode, whatever you want to call it.

After that little fiasco they all came in. I don't know the precise number but there were eight or more staff, and the female nurse was brandishing a syringe. Well, here we go I suppose! I told her it was ok, I'd pull my Calvin Klein underwear down for her myself, which I did. Then it was goodnight dick for me, soon I would know nothing and the total headache for the staff would be in an induced sleep for I don't know how long.

I woke up lying on that blue mattress/padded bed whatever, with the light streaming in. I hadn't even noticed there was a slit window in the back wall. I got up sheepishly and walked towards the wall. I then climbed onto the top of the padded chair to have a look. It was glorious sunshine outside! What was this, a cell? Was I in prison? Was I a criminal? No, I wasn't, and this place, albeit bad, wasn't any of the previous either, I knew that much! Here we go, round two!

I kicked off again, having to resort to shouting and bawling since there wasn't really anything else to do. Once again, they all came in after a while and jabbed me for a second time. Robert said he rang and rang and all they would say was that I was still in solitary confinement. It felt like forever, he said, then they would tell him again not to worry and that I was ok. He said that he prayed I would just behave and get out of there. In total I was in solitary confinement for seventy-two hours.

CLAIRE HALL

Second time I came around I just thought, in for a penny or a pound, I'm just going to have to behave because I just needed out of there. I remember they gave me some toast and tea. I ate and drank it like the good patient I was.

At some point that day I got out, and freedom never felt so good, even if I was still in a locked unit. They gave me a room, and it was ok. It had a window out onto the middle courtyard, although it was fixed, it didn't open. A bed with a plastic mattress, one pillow, one doorless wardrobe, one bedside cabinet, a sink without a plug, just in case any of us wanted to flood the place. It would be liveable I thought. Across from me was a huge bathroom with the biggest bath I had ever seen. I loved it. Down the corridor to the right of my room, towards the entrance doors, was the nurses' station, not like any I had seen before, it was all closed in with windows and a door. Opposite to that was a small day room, with sofas and a TV, and round the corner from the nurses' station, just before the entrance doors, was the drugs room – I would find that out later.

Staff just seemed to mull about and I thought, what sort of jobs are these, they get paid for nothing, or so I thought. To the left of my room down the corridor were some more bedrooms, a shower room, and an old-fashioned hood on the wall where a telephone had once been. At the very bottom was a large day room, then a dining area with an industrial kitchen next door, after that I think it was where solitary confinement was – been there got the T-shirt thanks very much.

To my amazement when I opened the drawers in the kitchen cupboards there was a whole set of cutlery, knives, I couldn't believe it. Why my train of thought went there I don't know. Probably to eliminate all the risks, after all, I was with all these mentally unwell patients, but I was different, I had a real reason for being unwell. After all, it just grief!

First thing I thought was could I go out for a tab. I went straight to the nurses' station, only to be informed that I wasn't allowed to go outside yet. What's that about? I'm totally behaving myself and it still isn't making any difference. I had a vape but frig that, I wanted to go outside and have a real cigarette. The patients, who by the way I wasn't one of, were going out. I would show them that I was different, for some reason they weren't getting it. I had no doubt in my mind that this was all a big mistake, and I was going to prove it to them. Why didn't they already know it? I didn't have the first clue why.

So, I decided to find the sanest patient to chat to, that would pass some time. Leanne (her name I learnt later), she would do! She wasn't pacing, or staring into space, or standing outside the drugs cupboard, she was just sitting on her bed in her room with the door open on her phone. "Hi," I said, "I'm Claire, thought I would introduce myself." Straight away she said come in and patted the bed for me to sit down. We got talking like old friends. She was easy to talk to and I liked her instantly. I've always known within minutes if I like someone or not.

Her story I soon found out was pretty awful. She'd had a terrible childhood and as a last resort she took herself to a flyover bridge, over a really busy motorway, and threw herself off. Thank God no car hit her, but because of the height she fell from she broke all the bones in her feet and legs, fractured her pelvis and broke a few ribs. She showed me the scars and they were horrific, probably like the ones in her mind, I thought.

I had an idea of what would make it better. I had some beautiful gold slippers, they were a Norwegian brand, Robert got me them as a Christmas present. They would make her feel better and they would miraculously make her feet and legs feel better too. I told her to wait a second. I wanted to give her something, so I went straight to get them from my room.

When I returned and gave her them she thought they were beautiful, and they were! She also loved the fact that they were natural sheepskin as her feet were always cold. She put them on, and it was like the story of Cinderella. Only instead of getting the prince, her legs and feet would be healed, which I thought was even better!

INTO THE BLUE

Chapter four
New home

INTO THE BLUE

Right! My room here is now my castle and I have to make it fitting. Everything is literal, has to be done instantly or thereabouts, as circumstances allows that's pretty much how I've always rolled. A mixture between the way I am and how I was brought up. Both my parents were doers, you see. My dad especially. Anything that needed doing had to be done there and then, also anything we owned had to be lovingly looked after. I think that comes from him being born during the time of the great depression.

Robert obviously had to get me some bits. He had done well – he brought me a lovely yellow night light, which went with the teddy bear he also bought because he had a black and yellow striped T-shirt on. All my cards, nicknacks and my very important tonic water were laid out on my chest of drawers, then of course all my clothes were hung up neatly in the doorless wardrobe, still haven't figured that out. I wanted a matching quilt cover, but Robert drew the line at that one!

I felt at ease now once the room was decked out, I could relax and enjoy being there. I almost forgot, but then remembered and asked that my most important item be brought in, my Bose speaker. It was small but remarkably loud and it was blue, it was meant to be. Sorted first night in my new abode, I was laying on my bed taking it all in when there was a knock on the door. I opened my bedroom door to a formidable nurse. I can say that for sure as I've met her type many times during my long service in the NHS. Later I would find out her name was Glenda, and I was right, she wasn't to be messed with.

Glenda wanted to know why I didn't want my nighttime meds. I told her no one offered me them, to which she said,

"Well you should be coming to the drugs cupboard for them," like I should have known that all along. I told her I was undecided whether to have them or not, to which she said it was up to me, but I may regret it later. Off she went. I thought about it for a little while and ended up making my mind up to take them that night but if they were in any way awful, I just wouldn't have any more, after all I probably didn't need them, I felt fine.

To the drugs cupboard I went, and there was a bit of a queue. This was *One Flew Over the Cuckoo's Nest* in real life. I worked up in the main hospital and yeah, ITU was different to the wards because drugs were given intravenously, but all the wards, in every hospital, all over England a nurse would come to each individual patient and give them their drugs. I hadn't ever seen this before. The film kept running through my mind as I was standing in line. How I didn't crack up I don't know, it was hilarious to me.

Down the hatch, back to the room, cleaned my teeth, lay on the bed, woke up to the light of the morning gleaming through the paper-thin curtains. Punch-drunk was the only way I can describe how I felt, groggy fog-like head, no I didn't like this one iota. I tried to pull it together. I went across the way and started running the bath, which would probably take hours, it was huge. Lots of bubbles, took my speaker over, why not, I do that at home. Among the array of toiletries that were brought in for me was my false tan and mitt, which I had the foresight to ask my nieces for as they understood, being women.

Ok, this will show them all, I thought, after my bath I'll put some false tan on and in an hour or so they will see how well

INTO THE BLUE

I am. The bath was so luxurious, and with my music playing and my clothes laid out, apart from the feeling of the drugs wearing off, I was going to make this a good day. They might even let me out for a smoke, you never know. Once out of the bath I lathered the false tan on, the darker the tan the healthier I would look, well that's what I was going for.

All done and still playing the music from my speaker, a pretty black girl came to my room door. She introduced herself, Maya was her name. She looked like an interesting person and during my stay there I found out she was. Maya was a music producer, singer, musician and an amazing artist. I got to know all that but never really got to know the reason why she ended up in a place like this. A breakdown maybe, I thought.

I loved her spontaneous personality. She was eccentric which I loved, I am the same. Over the following days I would either be in her room, or she would be in mine, flitting to see Leanne every now and then. Maya didn't really like that, she didn't mix and later I would find out she didn't like to share me either. I don't know why she was attracted to me, I think the music definitely first caught her interest. We later went on to forge a friendship, albeit a funny one.

At last! The answer was yes, I could go outside for a smoke. I couldn't retrieve my cigarettes and lighter from my room fast enough. They buzzed me out and away I went down the flights of stairs and then got buzzed out again. Aw, the fresh air, you forget how amazing it is. The first drag was a drawn-out affair as you can imagine. Don't know why but a tab is never better than when you're stressed, or maybe after sex, forgot about that, it had been a while. Outside there were not just women but men, never gave it a thought that there would be men who were unwell too and that they would have to have their own unit. My unit felt like an island off on its own, maybe that was to do with my mind or maybe it's because it's a locked environment, there's probably a lot to be said about that. I buzzed back in once I finished my smoke like it was perfectly normal, it never once entered my mind to do anything other.

I never really ate any meals while I was there. I'm not sure why. Robert used to bring me sushi most nights from Marks & Spencer as he was working nearby. He is a building construction site manager and was on a new build there. I was happy with the same thing daily, it gave me consistency which in some way made me feel like a normal human being.

That night I never went to the queue at the drugs room, and once again Glenda came to my door. I told her thanks but no thanks. She asked me why, so I told her honestly that I just didn't like the way they made me feel. I couldn't really explain the underlying thing I was trying to relay, though much later I would know: it was the nothingness, the way it relaxed you to such an extreme extent that you ended up with no personality of your own. You were just a body walking around in whatever clothing with no feelings either way about absolutely anything or anybody. She didn't put up a fight, a woman of her nature would never do that, she just told me frankly and honestly of the medical repercussions I may feel. I didn't know what she meant until that night. I watched the clock, every second of every hour, my mind racing but empty at the same time. She was right of course, I was quite seriously unwell at that present time, and I did need them. The next night I queued like everyone else. I had come to realise that I'd rather take the backlash of the drugs the next morning than have a torturous night with no sleep. Glenda never flinched, didn't say a thing, I did like her!

I started to notice all the different characters, their little quirks or their antics as the case may be. There was Alice who just wandered around with Liz, Liz being the quiet chaperone. Alice was a handwasher, her hands raw up to her elbows as she had practically removed most of the layers of skin, they were all cracked, red and angry. Her clothes were immaculately clean and pressed on her body. Her poor hubby used to bring a holdall bag in daily with the new batch of freshly washed and army-style ironed clothes to keep up with changes. In the meantime, Liz would just follow her aimlessly and just watch the whole process without an opinion.

Then there was Michaela, truly beautiful inside and out. Every day she wore a completely different outfit, one more fancy than the other. Yeah, she might have looked better placed on the set of *Dynasty*, but boy did she pull it off. I waited impatiently every morning for her to come out of her room to see what she was wearing that day. The corridor of our rooms was her entrance and the area in front of the nurses' station was her stage. She would parade, albeit timidly, for a couple of hours and then retreat back to her room and sadly sit for hours on her own in front of her chest of drawers that was overrun with jewellery, make-up, brushes, mirrors, perfumes, thinking that if she changed the outside, somehow the inside would be changed too. I will never forget the sadness behind her eyes even though she was just too much of a beautiful person to ever show it or say.

Mary, Mary whose door had a written message on it, 'Prayer in process do not disturb'!!! I had a feeling that I should probably be afraid! When I first laid eyes on her, by God I realised that was true, she was one big stature of a woman, as broad and tall as a huge man. No one, not even staff, seemed to speak to her, she would only come out to go outside for a cigarette and then march straight back into her room. I followed suit with everyone else. I wouldn't have dared to do any other, I didn't even want to cross paths with her in the corridor, never mind anything else if the truth was told. I can remember thinking if she kicks off, all hell will break loose. I would just have to barricade myself in my room, as there weren't many other options.

There was Viv, Viv whose eyes were as black as her hair. She had a severe crew cut, slim figure, always dressed smartly, almost like she was about to go to work somewhere important. Literally she just stood all day in front of the nurses' station like she was waiting for someone. Odd times she would approach staff who came out. I don't know what was said but the conversations were always short, and nothing came of them. Viv would have looked more normal on a category A landing. If I had been told she had murdered someone in her past I wouldn't have been shocked by it. I have to say she never caused any trouble, she never mixed with anyone, just kept to herself to herself, but I continued to stay wary of her.

Marie was anorexic (sorry about that description, but it was true), she was painfully thin to look at and avoided mealtimes at all costs. It was hard to hold a conversation with her without staring at her gaunt face or bony hands. Sadly, she was another lovely person again with problems that haunted her so deeply she couldn't control her thoughts so she controlled what went into her body, or should I say what didn't! We chatted quite often, sitting on her bed. She loved company and didn't seem to like being alone. Her bedroom was childlike, I didn't mind it, I quite liked it, although it was strange for a grown woman. The cover she had on her quilt was something a small child would have had.

Then there was Ayesha, spoilt, beautiful but also lost, her poor father looked worried sick every time he visited her. I say spoilt because she went on ridiculously after an overnight home stay only to find when she came back the next morning her room had been given to someone else. She paced the place in temper dressed in her black hijab, just her gorgeous eyes on show. I remember thinking if I was that stunning, I definitely wouldn't be in a place like this that's for sure! At the finish I was so sick of the carry-on I asked her to come into my room, which reluctantly she did. She asked me for a cigarette, as by that time I was having the odd one in my room. I bartered with her on the understanding that she calmed down. She agreed. I shut the door and we smoked and chatted. Close up I was taken back by her beauty, why did she not know this.

Finally for now there was Maya again, the talented, mysterious, clever Maya. She was one of the first patients to approach me, she had just come into my room like we were long-lost friends. Strangely I grew to want that to be true. Maya was a complete puzzle to me, although very interesting she was also complicated, I think that was the real draw. For some reason I've always been attracted to complicated or eccentric people, maybe because I'm one too, I don't know. I was later to find out Maya liked you all to herself, she absolutely did not want to share a friend.

CLAIRE HALL

So, Maya and I knocked around together in the unit, a bit like we were at high school only we slept there and couldn't leave, but it all felt perfectly normal. We would spend hours in each other's rooms. Maya's room was a tip when I first went in, I took the role as parent and told her I would only come back in if she tidied it up. There was a mountain of clothes on the floor, dirty underwear etc, and her bed was the same. I wondered if she just got in it the way it was. Lo and behold, not long after there was a knock on my room door and there she was like a small child wanting to give the good news, she had tidied her room. So of course I went over to do the inspection. "Marvellous, well done," I said. It wasn't exactly my standard, but it was night and day to the before. This was cause for a celebration as we were both chuffed, so we sat down on her newly tidied bed and looked through all her artwork. As a sort of prize slash incentive for tiding her room I gave her one of my favourite-smelling Febrezes. Can't stand the stuff now, not because it evokes any memories or anything, because even now, I look back on my time in the psychiatric unit with great fondness. She kindly gave me some of her artwork to put up in my room. I was so chuffed with it that I took it straight over with Maya to put it up on my walls, debating like you would in your home on where to place it. I loved it and thought it made my room come to life. We then lay on my bed just looking and admiring it for ages. I suppose looking back without disclosing anything at all about our past lives and the reason for even being there we just got each other. I like to think because I can't speak for her that we both knew silently that we each had great qualities that we instinctively loved about each other. The only difference being that I could be friends with everyone, well almost, bar Mary and Viv, but Maya couldn't. Even when I introduced her to my visitors, she didn't seem to like it and would leave and go back to her room.

My morning ritual was to go straight over from my room to the bathroom to bag it by laying out my clothes and my toiletries and of course my speaker. I needed to have music playing all the time. Once out of the bath, the false tan would be applied in substantial amounts again. I wanted to look as healthy and normal as I possibly could. Then some casual clothes because I wanted to be comfy too, as well as my lovely bracelet with the one blue heart left. It was the one Robert had bought for me for Blue's funeral, and it originally had two hearts but can you believe it one fell out and got lost during his service. Right, I was ready for the day, here we go!

Ideally, I would have liked to speak with all the patients on a daily basis but sometimes that just wasn't possible. After all I may be able to help them in areas where the consultant psychiatrist couldn't. My main obstacle was not upsetting Maya, which was pretty impossible if I wanted to do the above. Half the time I would try to squeeze a few in early before she got up as she liked to lie in bed late, which was good for me.

So, with Maya's door still closed I spotted Liz and Alice and went straight over. Liz said a quiet hello with Alice following. I was checking Alice's hands as we spoke, to see the extent of her recent damage. They were terrible but they weren't bleeding thankfully. We talked about all the things that you may talk to a stranger in the street about, small talk, weird I know but that's what we did. I needed to be inventive and come up with a way to get her out of this obsessive behaviour. It may even kill two birds with one stone because her poor husband would get a reprieve also. You could tell all the time she stood chatting she was thinking of being at the sink so she could relieve her feelings of being dirty. That's why I sort of knew there was no point having a deeper conversation. I don't think there was room in her mind for it! How mad is the human mind to allow OCD to get to such a level that you need to be sectioned and that all those thoughts and feelings literally take over one's mind. To end up living a life that's not even your own, where nothing else matters, only the actions that involve cleaning, cleaning yourself and being clean and if that doesn't happen the world will end! Your loved ones just having to watch from the sidelines hoping and praying for some sort of miracle to save you from your own mind.

I met Maya's family for the first time. They were very lovely, very bohemian, both were white so I didn't really understand that bit, but I would never have asked, maybe one was a step-parent. You could tell they adored her and vice versa. I loved seeing people's families come in. It was like a part of the missing jigsaw puzzle. Of course, some got visitors more frequently than others, and that really bothered me for some reason. I can remember thinking aha! That's why such and such is the way they are. Obviously, my background at the hospital must have aided me being confused about the whys and wherefores of me being there most of the time. For the main part I honestly thought I was there to help! To understand and maybe figure out the patients when no one else could, because after all they were all still here and I guessed it wasn't the first time for some of them. Then the mystery of me being there was then solved, that was it! It had to be!

INTO THE BLUE

All the time I was on high alert listening for key things in what they were saying and watching their behaviour the entire time. Most people's body language will tell you more than what comes out of their mouths. My job in Rehab for ITU patients at first mostly involves figuring out if the patients were a glass half full or half empty, optimist or pessimist, then a bit of background, like if they were a go-getter or not. Their ability to walk again, eat again, their mood, personal cares, communication are all secondary. This was the most important information because it was key to how their recovery would go. Me and my partner in crime, so to speak, the lovely Sonia, would take turns in playing good cop, bad cop. As you can imagine after weeks, sometimes months on Critical Care they are more than spent, so it takes a lot of kidology and gentle or firm persuasion to get them to Rehab. Our main concern and goal are to get the patient somewhere near to the person they were before their illness and ITU addmission.

Twenty years of caring for people like that ends up embedded into your whole being, whether you know it or not. I was always good with the most complicated patients. I remember from being small I've always had a deep interest in understanding people and how they tick. I would want to know or ask all sorts of things, the more the better. I can't really explain where it all came from, me coming to be like that, but I just know that as long as I can remember that's the way I was. So now that was my whole mission for being there and I would prove I was worth my salt in the process.

This one particular morning the beautiful Michaela came from her room in all her regalia. She could put it all together like no one else. Her blouse was so intricate, Edwardian in style, and she'd paired it with a gorgeous red skirt. Of course all the jewellery and make-up were intact, not a hair out of place. Like every morning, I told her how much I loved her outfit and how good she looked, I truly meant it. This time though I asked if I could take a photograph, not to scare her I said just of her outfit. She sheepishly agreed, but when I started taking some photos she looked secretly pleased and liked it, I think. I wasn't prying and never would I ever impose myself on anyone. I know I said before about my interest in people, but people saw it for what it was: genuine and honest; it was innocent and pure, and I was just as honest and free back with them.

So, photos taken I showed her for her kind of consent, you know, like if you were on a photoshoot and you are editing, like that. She loved them and I swear I saw a glimmer of confidence in her eyes. For all her dressing up and glam I could tell that it was her facade to hide her real feelings. I was chuffed, so was she. She went into her room and came out with a beautiful necklace and said she wanted me to have it. For all it was very lovely it would have looked totally out of place on my neck, not like on hers where it would look stunning. I thanked her but tried to insist that there was no need and that it was too much. She wouldn't accept it and said she wanted me to have it and that was that. All I could do then was thank her. I still have it now, it's something I will never part with.

Once on my own in my room I frantically phoned Robert to ask him to get the only thing I could think of, a *Vogue* magazine, yeah that would do! Later when Robert arrived at visiting time, I couldn't wait to get it from him and present it to her. I knocked and when she came to the door, I placed it out in front of my arms. She gasped like I had given her the Crown

INTO THE BLUE

Jewels, she was gleaming like it was her new prized possession. I was made up by her reaction and told her that I thought she should be in the magazine, which I very much meant. I left her gazing at it and holding it in her arms like a newborn baby and I went back to my room to have the rest of my visit with Robert.

Later, I went back to her room, and she beckoned me to come in. We then both sat on her bed and looked through the magazine page by page picking out what we thought would suit each other or things that we liked. I'm not sure how many hours passed but we spent ages over it, and I don't know who enjoyed it the most. I like a bit of *Vogue* in my life and have a penchant for designer shoes and clothes. When I was in one of my fast modes before my section it all got slightly out of hand. The fastness, that was something else!

Here's a taster: prior to this little stay in the psychiatric unit, I had some – habits, should we say? They got out of control two-and-a-bit years earlier when my mam died. Before her death I was as good as gold, yeah, I liked nice things and had a few but I had no debt, in fact I was a saver, then all hell broke loose. Didn't help I had no concept of money at all at the time, good job really because I spent it like water, but more on that later.

My mam died and I got fast, as in manic. I thought it was just the fact that I loved her more than life itself, never having a cross word in my entire life with her. I was fast by nature, but this was super charged, on a total other level. I just presumed it was grief and so did everyone else. As in manic, I mean two, three hours sleep a night and I was done, in fact it was hard work just to get that much. No time for food or anything, nope, I was far too busy for that. You may wonder how I got away with it. Well, in the days leading up to her funeral my partner knew the way I loved her with all my being, so he just put it down to that and after the funeral he went back to work away down south.

So, me and Bertie, that is Bertie my handsome but stubborn Fox Terrier, who luckily adored me and somehow knew instinctively that I was sad and needed him, walked miles upon miles over the coming months. If it was two, three in the morning that didn't matter, I would wrap up, it was November after all, he would get his coat on which he hated with a passion and then his leader and off we went. There was never any purpose to our walks, we weren't walking to get somewhere, as you've probably gathered keeping them hours! That didn't deter me, my mind was busy, busy all the time and every thought was a matter of urgency and of the utmost importance.

If I was to describe it to you it's like being in a permanent fight or flight mindset with no break, like an animal and their instinctive nature. That's why they are so quick in their responses because the nature of the beast, for want of a better expression, is instinctiveness. In order to do that they live only in the moment, not troubled by the past or future. You may be thinking that's terrible but there are, I believe, some extraordinary qualities to it, even though I'm not recommending it either, ha!

So, for example I would notice the smallest of things and appreciate every aspect of it, good or bad. Nature, for instance – obviously I saw a lot of it on my many walks, the colour of the leaves, the way the trees swayed in the wind, the rain and OMG the snow! I was in awe of everything that I encountered, objects, places, people, anything. It was like being reborn with a fresh set of eyes; why had I not seen any of it before, I can remember wondering. Like animals I was not troubled by the past or the future, in fact for the most part I feel guilty for saying I forgot my mam had died. There was no hiding any of my behaviour though, I couldn't have even if I tried, and if I had had the choice in my mind I wouldn't have taken it anyway. So, all the usual drudge that weighs you down I didn't have, and this is how my mind could operate on such an astonishing super-charged, super-fast level depending on how you look at it.

Now this to me is the extraordinary bit, my mind was in total freedom, a freedom that normal functioning humans in the main cannot be privy to ever! Because they are not able to switch off from the worries of the past or the future. But it can also be dangerous as fear is eradicated from your mind, for without the past you don't know fear. There is one more danger, it can be very addictive, almost like a drug. After all that's why addicts are addicts – because they like to be out of their own mind and in a total freedom far from the reach of the thoughts they are tortured by. I believe that's why so many people who experience the mania like it, but mania comes with an avalanche of a downside, down being the optimum word. What goes up must come down and, for example, only two weeks of mania can lead to a year's depression. But back to the up note: it's amazing how much people will go along with you when they are slightly fearful or do not understand your behaviour. Overall, they will not make an already difficult situation for you any worse. It would be more than apparent that something was wrong if you spoke to me long enough.

Outings by a long shot though were a lot safer when just out on a walk with Bertie rather than by myself, i.e. going to shops etc. Going to shops meant a multitude of things that could go wrong. It was like being in a war zone trying to dodge bullets and minefields and the SPENDING! Then of course internet shopping, I spent about twenty grand that time round! But more about that later, that's probably a whole book in itself!

Chapter five
Therapy plans and wedding plans

Day four/five in the Big Brother house, I have no tally of the days as you can imagine but I've tried my best to put them in some sort of order.

This particular day in the Tranwell, one of the HCAs, Aditi, was on duty. She was of Indian origin, and you could just tell she had a lovely nature about her, it was in her whole aura. She mentioned to me and Maya that she did henna, and we were overjoyed to hear this and straight away asked her if she would do it for us. There we were not long later sitting in the day room getting our arms and hands done. She asked if I wanted anything specific in the pattern and I asked her to put the name Blue. So very gently she asked why Blue, so I informed her that it was the name of my deceased son. She looked shocked and visibly upset. She carried on with a touch as light as a feather and by the time she was finished it was beautiful. All the stunning henna patterns surrounding Blue's name. I was amazed and couldn't thank her enough.

When it was Maya's turn everyone came for a look and by the time she was finished, Aditi had a flurry of patients wanting theirs done, but for two exceptions, Alice and Liz. Maya's henna was so intricate she was automatically in love with it and then one by one Aditi started working her way through the now substantial queue. This was going to be a whole day's work, but I must admit everyone was patient and there was an air of happiness probably because it was a gift, a gift from Aditi.

Everyone walked around all day and night with their arms and hands in midair, on parade but also for a practical reason as no one wanted to smudge them. We took turns admiring each other's henna, oohing and ahhing at each one. It was certainly a sight for sore eyes.

Well then, the predicament came, bedtime! What was I going to do now? Yeah it was ok getting in, at first I would just keep it out of the quilt, but if I fell asleep what would happen then? I didn't shut my eyes all night. In reality nothing would have happened to it, but my mind doesn't operate like that, even normally. I was shattered the next day but had to get on with my morning ritual, except today I sat with my arm as far out of the bath as I could manage and there would be no false tan applied that day.

Everyone must have had a similar idea, as on close inspection everyone's henna was intact and looking good, great result. We were becoming a little team I thought, united by henna. Well, this was the first step, I thought, we should keep going with this united front, I would just have to come up with a plan first to keep the momentum going!

There was another HCA who was lovely too, her name was Suzanne. Well, I got talking to her and it turned out she could paint nails and she said there was a stash of nail varnishes somewhere. So we went on the hunt and found a whole variety of colours. I even found a foot spa, still in the box. Right, that was it! This would be the plan B, a Spa Day! It was all going to go swimmingly, and everyone had to get involved.

INTO THE BLUE

I asked Suzanne to enrol Aditi and anyone else with the appropriate talents. I got on with the mammoth task of getting all or the majority of the patients to agree to attend. We would hold the event in the small day room I thought, it would need a fair bit of tidying and cleaning beforehand. I remember wanting everyone to be as excited for it as I was. That didn't seem to be the case and I had no idea why; all they did all day was wander from one room to another or along the landing. What was wrong with these people?

Anyway, I wasn't going to let that stop me from making headway. I had a list of jobs to do before the event the next day and it might just be that they were saving their excitement for tomorrow. Maya and I cleaned and tidied the day room, although her cleaning left a lot to be desired, her lack of enthusiasm in that department showed. Once the room looked as good as it was going to get – as you may imagine the last thing on prior patients' minds was looking after it or anything else for that matter – we started laying out everything. The nail varnishes we lined up in order of shades, you know like a real salon, clean NHS towels neatly folded, foot spa at the ready, we even went as far as putting water bottles out for all of them. I couldn't wait for them to see it; all we were missing was a red ribbon and a pair of those gigantic scissors!

I'm embarrassed now to admit I never asked Mary to attend, I was still too afraid and unable to pluck the courage up to ask. I also gave someone else the job of asking Viv, after all that's what people do when hosting, they must delegate. Beautiful Michaela loved the idea, she was a no-brainer, she would just have to spend a couple of hours taking off what she already had on. Then there was Leanne, she was hesitant because of all the scars on her feet, but I convinced her, and I meant it when I said it really didn't matter to anyone, and no one would care.

Ayesha was on a day visit at home, and I was gutted as she would have really loved it and she could have helped, after all that was her real vocation. I needed Alice to say yes as my numbers were looking poor and if she said yes Liz would automatically say yes too.

I had to give myself a motivational chat at the mirror in my room. How on earth would I get Alice on board? It was her number one fear, all that touching and sharing, I'd have to give a speech worthy of an inaugural address to her. Well here goes nothing! I could see her and Liz going into the big day room down the bottom of the unit. I swear my feet were dragging all the way, if I walked any slower, I would stop! I hated persuasion tactics with a vengeance. As I went into the day room I tried to switch my body language to confident and persuasive, rather than sheepish and lacklustre, which is harder than you think.

"Alice, Liz," I started, "I'm glad I caught you." Not like they were going anywhere in a locked unit but hey ho! "I want to invite you both to our wonderful spa day." Now for the hard sell. I cleared my throat and started. "Now before you say yes or no, I want you to listen to all the wonderful things we are going to be doing and all the benefits I might add." Not wanting to put too much emphasis on the nail handling or feet washing I sort of skirted around those things and added a few white lies, one whopper being that I had spoken to the consultant psychiatrist, and he said that this event had high rewards, as in the interaction with everyone and being in the same room all together was very positive. I emphasized the next bit, that he had also said we all must be doing things that are out of our comfort zones, pushing the boundaries where we can as it is advantageous for our recovery. Also, the added extra, when our loved ones found out they would be made up.

I waited with bated breath for their, her answer. All the time they both sat turning their heads every two minutes to look at each other, probably to see if the telepathy was working. After what seemed like days Alice came up with "I'm not sure." Eeee this was friggin mental, give me a break, after all I wasn't well either, how much persuasion did they think I had in me!

Last shot this time I was going firm all the way as my patience was waning. "Look, you both must come if the truth be told" I said, "it's part of our Rehab and the consultant wants to know the names and numbers of who attended afterwards." "Ok," she said reluctantly, and Liz followed with a yes. Bravo! I may not get to Heaven but at least this was now a done deal, probably my best achievement ever! I knew the anxiety would start from the moment she agreed but frankly I was too busy to think about it. She would have to get on with it. Normally I would be the first to want to help but just not at this present moment. Her chaperone Liz would have to aid her. I didn't have much faith in that happening but at least I could pretend for now.

Next morning all present and correct, it was like herding cattle but never mind it was eventually happening! At last! We all took our positions, patients sitting and HCAs at the ready to either paint fingernails or feet after the foot spa of course. So, plan devised we took our turns with the foot spa, myself and Maya making a point of changing the water and an even bigger deal of relaying that it had been disinfected and washed out between feet. Probably only for Alice's benefit, I doubt anyone else was bothered.

So here we all were sitting with our beautiful nail polishes on, mine being Blue of course! A rainbow of colours when I looked around the room. Maya's was funky to match her personality, everyone chose a different colour which was nice. When it came to Alice choosing her colour, she just said "I'll have any." To be honest I watched her and I just thought she's thinking 'hurry up, get it on and get it over with, so I can get back to my room to take it off.'

Michaela's was red of course, nothing else would have sufficed. Then we suggested the HCAs paint each other's nails while we were still taking it in turns with the foot spa. Tortuous is the only way to describe Alice's turn with the foot spa, Liz watching like you would when your child takes its first steps. It felt like the first moon landing, and she was Neil Armstrong, honestly when her feet slowly submerged into the water, I felt like crying out 'One small step for mankind.' How the frig did we pull this off? My mouth was agape the whole time, afraid to take a breath in case it put a mocker on the process.

But we had lift-off! Then we landed the rocket safely! And we even got the astronaut to say a few words afterwards. Amazeballs! Couldn't get over it, I think I was in shock. We might as well push the boat out now her feet were out safely and gently getting patted dry by the ever-adoring Liz, let's get them toenails painted. I gestured to Suzanne who totally got the drift and went straight over, displaying all the lovely nail polishes for Alice to choose a colour for her toenails. Alice chose and Suzanne painted them.

INTO THE BLUE

All done, I was mentally drained and felt completely shattered, I hope they all bloody appreciated it. We would have to wait for another team get-together for now. I needed to put my feet up and chill, I certainly wasn't hanging my hat up yet, just for now!

That same evening Alice's nail varnish was gone like the wind, like it never happened. It was probably straight after, but I never saw her until later as I had to have a nana nap to get over the day's events. Never mind new day tomorrow! In the meantime, everyone had congregated down in the big day room for whatever reason. I couldn't help myself, knowing full well my intent when I went down. I said hello to everyone, not leaving any stone unturned, then I proceeded to make myself comfy on one of the settees.

In the meantime, I was clocking the room. Alice was desperately trying to sit on her hands, not with much luck, because her brain wouldn't allow her to put them there. Liz sitting beside her was looking shifty. I was glad though to see Maya there as it wasn't usually her thing at all. Maybe today did do some good, Maya was mixing! Viv was out on the landing as usual, and Mary was either praying or smoking.

"Well," I said, "did everyone enjoy today?" I knew the feedback would be piss-poor but continued anyway. "I thought it was great personally," deliberately showing off my fingernails and toenails in my flip flops. Maya thank God was enthusiastic, she loved it and said she would want to do it again maybe even next week. Slightly early for me but never mind, on to the next. Marie thought it was great and even wore a matching pink-coloured outfit to really show them off. I informed the group I had called in on Leanne in her room on my way down and she was really happy about the whole day. Without any need to say, everyone knew Michaela was made up and that it had probably made her year never mind week.

I waited and waited until I eventually couldn't keep it in any longer. "Alice, Liz, did you two enjoy it?" I gave up! The two of them didn't even know how to reply, one looking at the other for help, so I helped them instead. I stood up and said that today I thought they had done things that nobody would have ever believed they would do, even themselves, nobody would have thought it possible. So, to me that was not only momentous but probably not much short of a miracle and if they put their mind to it there was no limit to what they could achieve. As I was leaving, I also added "It's only your mind that's stopping you achieving more things like you did today." Off to bed I went. They could make of that what they wanted, I was too wrecked to care.

Bright and early feeling refreshed from the day before I did my usual ritual in the bathroom, this time plucking up the courage to apply false tan, just a gentle dusting near my henna tattoo. Back in my bedroom it was like a bolt of lightning hit me from the sky, me and Robert should get married! I thought about it for probably three minutes or so and then the panic set in. I needed to find a dress, shoes, venue etc, etc.

I went straight on my phone. As I mentioned before, my little hobby was going to come good today as I knew exactly the websites to start my search. Net-a-Porter, Matches.com, Browns, not fussed about Harrods website and although I love Selfridges so much I could move in tomorrow, their website leaves a lot to be desired, I thought. I trawled for ages but couldn't really see anything I liked. You must remember money in my mind or in my bank account wasn't really a concept at this present time or in the world for all I knew.

Maya came to my room which was a welcome break from the searching, though I didn't mention it to her for now. I wanted to keep a lid on it, at least until I found the dress. She wanted to show me the lyrics she had written for a song down in the activity room. It was strange being that far down the bottom of the corridor, as the activity room was right next door to the solitary confinement room. It made me think about all the people who had gone nuts in there like me. Like the dungeons in the castles of far-gone days where people went mad, totally losing their mind and then their battered blood-soaked bodies would be found on the stone-covered floors.

Maya's voice brought me back into the room, and instead of her talking through her lyrics I asked her to sing them. WOW what an amazing voice she had, so natural, sultry, jazz-toned, I was blown away! You could tell she was a pro. There was no hesitation, confident but relaxed, she sang with an ease that I think you are either born with or not. She sang and I clapped, I asked for an encore again and again, and she also sang a few of her other songs. Why oh why was she here? In this place! I couldn't get my head around it, it totally baffled me. On the outside she not only could have sung for her supper well and truly, but for everyone else's too for that matter. She could be sitting on a little gold mine; she could be minted!

Later in the day I made my excuses. I needed to get in my room and get cracking with everything cause at this rate there wouldn't be a wedding. Bearing in mind in the real world

Robert has no idea he is getting married, and I had no idea I was sectioned, and my abode was a locked psychiatric unit.

Door shut, straight on my bed, phone in hand, back on the hunt. Not sure how it happened but I stumbled across a website called My Self Portrait. I had heard of it on my many travels on the web but had never visited their site. Wow, there was an abundance of dresses to choose from, each one better than the one before. I hurriedly checked if they had accessories, i.e. shoes. Yeah, they did. I'd hit the jackpot!

I have a tendency depending where I am on the Richter scale of my mind at that present time, to also be super-fast while purchasing goods and I mean any! From a pencil to a small closet of clothing. I like what I see, stick it in the basket and carry on. But when I'm fast, I will get stuck on a website. Although I could purchase thousands of pounds of goods, my mind isn't capable of stretching to multiple tasks, like looking elsewhere. For example, like I mentioned before when my mam died, I went haywire. I don't think I said this bit though, I spent sixteen thousand pounds on the My Theresa website in about six minutes! I think I was looking for Gucci. I did get as far as the Gs but ended up spending the entirety on Givenchy, because GI came before the Gus. See what I mean about my mind's incapabilities and not to mention the danger!

So Self Portrait it was. I liked a few of them, but I eventually dwindled it down to one. My conundrum though was when I clicked on the dress the model had cowboy boots on with it and when I looked, they didn't even sell boots on their website. I racked my brain because on closer inspection I knew I had seen the boots before, but where that was, was the trillion-dollar question.

INTO THE BLUE

Never mind, I had the dress in the basket, so then I clicked onto their shoes and I saw a pair that would do, after all I may need bridal shoes too. Cream slip-ons with a kitten heel and diamante stones down one side, they had the exact same in black. What the hell, I put them in the basket too. But I needed an address. They couldn't go to mine and spoil the surprise, so I rang Sonia my colleague but also my friend. I told her of my intentions and asked could I please use her address, to which, with much apprehension, she said yes. I don't think she wanted to send me over the edge by refusing.

Now, I needed to find those cowboy boots. I racked my brain, kept looking and scanning the image on the screen, zooming in and out a zillion times. Then eventually I remembered where I had seen them, it was in Fenwick's Newcastle where I live, I had seen them when I was buying my funeral outfit. After Selfridges it's in my top ten department stores. I always think they should do sleepovers, I think they would go down a storm. My first time in London my partner and his cousin who lives there dropped me off at Selfridges while they went to the War Museum. I was under strict instructions not to deviate from the building, and they would ring my mobile on their return. Needless to say, from the hour of nine a.m. until four forty-five p.m., no drink passed my lips, no food, no pit stops or a sit down. I was in Heaven I thought, not knowing where to go first! It was like that 'Race Across the World' programme, only 'A Race Across A Department Store'! A satnav would have been wonderful.

A day or so later I was on it! Fenwick's website it is! Right, category, shoe, boots, all. Barely containing my excitement, I swear it must be like the feeling pirates had when they were searching for hidden treasure. I scrolled and scrolled, then there they were in all their glory. Now next question, did they have a size thirty-nine? Couldn't believe my luck they had my size, so now I needed to purchase them. I am so well versed in it all now that it has grown to be one of my best talents to date.

I couldn't find my bank card. I searched the whole room multiple times, where the hell was it? This was a nightmare. I had eventually found them and now someone else could buy them from literally under my feet if I didn't find my card. I rang my niece who had been in the day before visiting. I told her about not being able to find my card and she informed me that she was sure Robert had it. How could this be, I remember thinking, I obviously had it to buy the dress! Not knowing that because I had informed them that I had made a couple of purchases – not a wedding dress, just stuff – they had confiscated it and for good reason I may add.

What to do now? In my panic I thought, well maybe Fenwick's would have them in store and hold them for me if I acted important enough. All I needed was to buy some time, enough time to persuade someone, anyone to go over and purchase them for me. So, sitting on my bed, in the Tranwell, room door shut, I had to start getting into character, acting out the role to myself. After a few goes I thought there's nothing else for it! Just ring! "Fenwick's," the operator answered, "which department?" "French Salon," I replied, that's where a shoe of their calibre would be.

"Hello, French Salon, how can I assist you?" Here we go. "Hi, I was wondering if you had the new season Ganni half cowboy boot in please, size thirty-nine." "Hang on, I'll just check that for you," came the reply from the very helpful sales assistant. After a few minutes she came back on and gladly informed me that yes, they did have them in stock but that they only had one pair left in store and can you believe it in my size! Don't know who was more excited about that prospect, her or me!

This was when I got into character, more like Jack Nicholson in *The Shining* but never mind. "Well actually I was wondering because I have back-to-back meetings all day if you would hold them for me, please." I waited while she got her reply in order. "Ordinarily," she started, "that would not be a problem but because they are the very last pair, we could only hold them for a few hours". Well, that was no good. I know I can be pretty persuasive but this time it just wasn't working.

I tried one more time to stretch it out until the next day, stating that there was no possible way I could get over today, but no, she wasn't having any of it, so I had to give up the ghost and thanked her for her time. Had to keep the CEO demeanour going until the end of the call.

With cowboy boots on my mind, I tried my level best to get on with my day. I mulled about like a lovestruck teenager all day, all over them bloody boots. Later that day to satisfy my needs I rang the social club. That went tickety-boo thank goodness, and the date was set for the do. I have no idea now of the date that never happened, but it was late summer that year, that's all I remember. A couple of days later my friend Sonia rang my mobile and asked if it was ok to visit that day as my dress and shoes had arrived. "Yes of course," I said, I couldn't wait!

There we both were in my room for the grand unboxing; the shoes could wait, the dress was first priority. As the dress unfolded in my arms, I could see all the intricate detailing on the silk material. To be honest that was the only thing that sold it to me, that one minor detail. The style of dress was inconsequential to me, it was really for someone with no bust, or double As and unfortunately, I had a pair of double Fs. But when my head is like that, I always buy with someone else in mind, figure that one out cause I'm still trying! I was also incapable of knowing my sizing at that time, probably No Shit Sherlock because I had ballooned. Looking back, my eating habits may have come into it, but the antipsychotic meds never helped either!

Into the deep, I lifted the dress over my head, still wearing my tracksuit! Arms in and pulled it down. I did think eee! It fits! Although I did have another layer of clothing underneath, I was more than happy with that. Sonia on the other hand, stood at the other side of the bed facing me in my tiny room, was mortified!

When I look back, I must have looked a right clip! But it was the action, the doing and the oh look at me sort of thing, I'm not poorly I've sorted a whole wedding myself for Christ's sake. Sonia on the other hand didn't know whether to laugh or cry! I asked her if she liked it. Lost for words for a while, then regaining her composure, she declared she wasn't sure! I think that's all she could muster to be fair.

On to the shoes, I was like Cinderella on a good day! Perfect fit, check! Club, sorted, check, dress which left a lot to be desired but check, boots nearly check. Once those cowboy boots were attained, I would be off down the aisle! And so would Robert!

INTO THE BLUE

Another day another dollar as they say, today's activity was an outing to Saltwell Park, how exciting! But what the frig, I might as well go. The PE trainer Donna came and informed us of the time and outline of the day. I mean, we were going for a walk around a park, but if she was going to make a meal of it like it was an expedition to the North Pole, who was I to disagree? I wondered who would be the Shackleton of the group.

So, a quick bath, more false tan for the day's event, it was lovely and sunny so leggings, T-shirt and flip flops it was. Got downstairs slightly earlier where we had to meet so I could have a cigarette. Here she came, our expedition leader, she had a slight frame but a big complex I thought. Bodies started to congregate, men as well. I don't know why I felt surprised by that, but I did. A couple of seven-seater taxis turned up and off we went.

Once we got to the park, I honestly thought it would be a leisurely stroll, take in the greenery, some sunshine, even sunbathing, after all it was the weather for it. Maybe an ice cream or a cup of tea but oh no, Donna had other ideas! She proceeded to march us around the park like it was a PT exercise. I'm a fast walker but even I found it hard to keep up with my flip flops. We passed a few dogs with their owners and to our own peril we stopped to stroke them. Well, the gap between us and the other half of our group that did not dare to stop was huge now. I was truly pissed off but would keep a lid on it for the sake of the group's morale.

Eventually catching up, breathless at this point, I won't stretch it out, it wasn't a sprint, but it wasn't far off! What a bitch she is! Then something caught my eye, a stunning tree with the park maze standing behind it, so I quickly got my phone out and clicked away, David Bailey style. Well then that was that, I saw something else I wanted to photograph and so on and so on. That's another trait I have in my mania, everything gets photographed, a sticker on a phone box, graffiti on a concrete slab, the more unusual the better and a lot of nature of course, as I'm normally outdoors – indoors I'm like a caged animal.

Then Dictator Donna came marching over to me: "You haven't got time to take photos," she barked. So, I stated the obvious and said I thought the whole point of coming to the park was to be in nature and to be able to soak it all in, not to run around it like you were in training for the Olympics! I swear I witnessed some steam coming out of her, she was foaming, how dare I question her professional being. Well, I had and that was that. She needed to remember I was the one on the edge!

She gave me some bollocks excuse about getting everyone from A to B as the only aim, and that was the end of our little jaunt. Didn't even get the friggin ice cream, back in the taxis to the Tranwell we went. Home sweet home.

That night Emma and Val came to visit me. Emma rang prior to say, so I took the opportunity to ask her to bring me some alcohol in like it was the most normal thing to do. She later informed me that she nearly had a nervous breakdown over that contraband offence. But she brought it anyway, that's the type of friend she is. So, in turn I saved her and Val a Cornish pasty off the tea trolley, they were lush. Val declined but me and Emma wolfed ours down with lashings of tomato sauce. I washed mine down with the can of gin and tonic that Emma very kindly brought in.

I showed the two of them round, introducing people along the way, and they seemed very impressed. Back in my room I told Val I loved her Hennessy T-shirt so much so we ended swapping tops, and I was well chuffed. Well, this had been a very productive visit I thought, we must do it again. Val loved my room, she said she thought it was so cosy and laughed as she said "I could stay here!" She could for me but I'm not top and tailing, she would have to get her own room. When it came time for them to go, I waved them off like you would from your own front door.

I had an abundance of visitors, from friends from home to family and my work colleagues of course. Some of my work colleagues came during their break on the unit, hence they were in uniform. One of the sisters from my unit, my boss, Tracy, came while on shift. I was smoking outside when she came walking down, so of course I took her on the unit and showed her around like I did with everyone who came to visit. Showing her all the rooms, my bedroom, activity room, even the kitchen, I had to show her the knife drawer to see if it shocked her as much as it did me.

It's funny that your mind has the capacity to compartmentalise things you want to know and the things you don't. For instance, with the knives thing I obviously comprehended I was in a secure unit then, but when it came to my understanding of why I was there it was absolute denial, I was just there by some mistake, but madly also content to stay.

Luckily Tracy knew me, and we had an unspoken respect for one another. She had been there through my whole journey after my mam's brain aneurysm, me then becoming her carer with my dad and then her death. But most of all she had a deeper understanding than most of my new gigantic void that sadly can never be filled, the death of my child. I will always be eternally grateful for all her empathy and kindness.

This particular day I was busying myself in my room, Maya had been in and out as she did. When she left, I put my music on, which was mostly always on, but once on my own I turned up the volume on my speaker. I heard a voice passing my open-door shout "Nina Simone." I quickly ran to my door to see who it was. I couldn't believe the figure walking away, it was friggin 'Mary'! The very same 'Mary' who never uttered a solitary word to anyone, the very same 'Mary' who we were all shit frightened of! So, I shouted back "Which one?" and she replied without looking back "'Lilac Wine'."

Well, I never saw that coming. I didn't know how quick to get on Spotify to find the song, which to my recollection I had never heard before, even though I had an eclectic taste in music and a vast amount saved in my library. I found it! Then sat nervously at the ready with it on pause as I waited with bated breath on her return from her usual morning tab.

I was trying to be as incognito as possible as I stuck my head around my door to see if she was coming back on the unit. More like Peter Sellers in the Pink Panther movies rather than a supersleuth. I don't really know how successful I was, but eventually there she was, coming towards me. She didn't really have an option as her room was down from mine. Like every good DJ I pressed play, full blast on cue. I couldn't see her reaction as I had to pretend to be far too busy in my doorless wardrobe doing something. I figured this was the best way forward as she was defo not an any attention at all type!

I put a few more Nina Simone tunes on, guesswork as I didn't know her music that well. Then I turned it down as I didn't want to seem too keen, didn't want to scare her off and put a stop to our newfound common ground. Well at least now I knew music was the key to her heart, which when you think about it, it's virtually impossible not to be able to find a song that evokes a memory in someone. I stayed in my room knowing her habitual smoking would come into play again and it wouldn't be long before she passed again to go outside.

Moses parted the seas and Mary came out of her room onto the corridor. I waited until she just got past my door, and I shouted, "Which song next?" to which she replied, "'I Put a Spell on You." She certainly had, I was now at her total beck and call and would pander to her every whim! Hence on her return 'I Put a Spell on You' played loudly from my speaker. What was going through her mind, I thought as it played, hopefully enjoyment. New friend, check! Well maybe that was slightly zealous of me but it's always good to live in hope.

Later that day I went outside for a cigarette and God answered my prayers, Mary landed while I was taking a drag. To my utter astonishment she came and stood next to me, towering over me as she lit her cigarette. I desperately sought to find the right vocabulary before I opened my gob. "Have you always liked jazz"? I asked. "Yes," was her firm reply and before I could panic about what would be my next sentence, she started rhyming off all the artists she liked.

I asked her to repeat them to me so I could quickly start putting them into my phone. I then suggested when we go back up (as we are now long-lost friends) that I play them, to which she agreed in her stern manner, that would do me. While I was on a good thing, I relayed all the older artists I like, and she seemed impressed. Who knew eh! Mary could talk! And moreover, she could socialise!

I finished my tab first and not wanting to spoil what we had going, I said I would see her upstairs to which she nodded. Not one person on the unit would believe what had just occurred, in a way I didn't want to say, as I had no intention of ruining it. I started to play her tunes and a new playlist was formed, Mary's playlist, and after all of that we went on to have numerous conversations and cigarettes, strictly only chatting while outside but that was good enough for me.

My lovely nurse Ruth informed me that there would be another outing tomorrow with Dictator Donna to the local nature park which was only a short distance from the unit. Would I give her one more shot or what? I told her I would think about it.

I just chilled out the rest of the day with Maya. We put face masks on and lay on her bed, laughing at how hilarious we looked. I did love being with her, I only wished she would be more open to the whole group. It's amazing how time flies in a place like that, but it does. It must have had something to do with how all our minds were, no one, not once ever tried to leave the whole time I was there. There is a certain clarity when your mind is free of all worries, past or present. On the outside people, me included before I was sectioned, think 'Aw, they're all nuts, they will have no recollection of anything, what would they know?' You would be amazed, this is exactly why I have a vivid memory of my time there, because basically I wasn't thinking about anything else!

I woke up to a beautiful morning. When I opened my curtains and looked at the blue sky I thought, go on then, I'll give the dictator one more chance. Bathed and tanned, I put trainers on as I wasn't getting caught with my pants down this time! We met outside again, and as per, my lot's attendance was piss-poor. Good job the lads' numbers were better.

There she was, Dictator Donna in all her regalia, all she was missing was a black and white striped top and a whistle. How she loved it, bet she got away with murder with some of the patients because she could always say "They aren't well, who you gonna believe?" twat!

I spotted one of the lads who was at Saltwell Park, so I asked him if he didn't mind if I walked with him. Well, I've never been shy, and he was as easy as an old shoe, of course he said yes. Off the group went, cutting through the hospital grounds, then across a road and then we were there. I was keeping an eye on how this was going to go down, wishing we'd had bets on. Sure enough off she trots, I'll rephrase that, off she gallops. Everyone was out of breath and getting prickled by all the millions of nettles every two feet, because there was defo no time to watch out for them. Dock leaves would have been just the trick, but unless David Attenborough was going to turn up, we had Bob Hope and no hope of easing the pain from them.

Halfway she let us stop for a water break – you know, the type of thing you do when you're climbing Ben Nevis, see what I mean! I had had enough. I am an actual walker/rambler, before all this I'd done it all my life, but this was beyond. Before she set off again, I asked if I could have a word. She ushered everyone on and hung back. "Look," I said "I don't understand why we are doing this again, racing around the fields instead of taking it all in and enjoying a leisurely stroll." She was mortified at the absolute cheek I had pulling her up once again, it was written all over her face, there was no hiding it. "Claire, why do you insist on trying to tell me how to do my job?" was her egotistical reply. I didn't expect anything less from her. So, like when you speak to a five-year-old, I told her in simplistic terms that was not my intention, all I was saying, for the second time, was could we just take our time and enjoy the 'nature!' at the Nature Park!

She followed it up with something like did I not want my lunch that day? I in turn I told her I didn't really have lunch, and when she asked why, I told her that Robert was working at his site down on the Team Valley, and he brought me sushi from Marks & Spencer most nights.

I thought there was something wrong with my hearing when I heard her reply. "Well lucky you, some of us aren't that spoiled and some of us haven't even got a significant other either." Eh what the fuck, is she joking or what? I've lost my friggin child! That was one of the very few times while I was there that my memory was triggered enough to remember my beautiful Blue was dead, never coming back. I wanted to put my hands around her neck and choke her until she had no breath left and see if she then felt as scared as I was, knowing that I had to live my entire life without him. I knew if I opened the lid of my mind just a touch more and let all my feelings come to the fore all hell would break loose. I would be arrested, and she would be a hospital case or worse. She wouldn't have to worry about getting back for lunch, she would never be eating again! And I would be spending the rest of my natural in Broadmoor!

How I reined myself in I have no idea, I had no words for her, nothing, only the thoughts swirling round my mind while I was looking at her. Eventually my feet did the talking and I just walked away from her. There was nothing else for it, other than borrowing a shovel from somewhere, hitting her hard and digging her a ditch to go in. I couldn't wait to get back to the unit away from her. Sprint she wanted, sprinting she got! I made my own way back to the unit quick smart! When I arrived back on the ward my nurse Ruth asked where everyone else was. Why was I alone?

So I told her that I had come back by myself and the exact reason why and I added what was going through my mind after she said what she said. Ruth looked pissed; I thought it was directed at me at first but no, it was at Double D. She asked if I was ok. I said I just wanted to go lie on my bed for five, to which she replied that sounded like a good idea and for me not to worry, she was going to deal with this.

Later that afternoon Gail the nurse in charge, in the navy, knocked on my door. She asked if I would tell her in detail of the day's events, only if I didn't mind doing so? So, I told her exactly what I had told Ruth earlier. Gail couldn't apologise enough and was so sorry that I had been put through all of what I had, in her mind due to the very inappropriate behaviour of a person who was supposed to be a professional taking care of us. Then she added that she would be speaking to that person ASAP and would get back to me tomorrow with a follow-up, to which I just agreed.

CLAIRE HALL

The knock on my door woke me the next morning. It was Double D Donna, double T really, for TOTAL TWAT. Without any hesitation she went into full-blown apology mode. To be honest, call me soft, I thought it sounded pretty sincere at first, but then she ended by saying although it was no excuse, she had just gone through a bad break-up with her partner and had been feeling really stressed. The latter for me she should have defo omitted, did I look like Jerry Springer? If she hadn't noticed I was myself in quite a peculiar predicament to say the least, I was locked in for the main part in a secure unit for my own protection. But never one to disappoint, I listened to the rest of her shite and said let's let bygones be bygones. Then off she went, and I put it to bed as soon as I shut the door. Suffice to say I wouldn't be attending any more trips out from now on in.

Chapter six
Prayer mats and a new admission

Ayesha's father came in to visit her that day with his stressed face intact. He just couldn't hide it, and I know that sounds cruel of me, but it used to send me over the edge. In my mind I just started to pre-empt things, because why else was he so worried unless something awful was about to happen? Not for one minute thinking something already had! He brought with him the most beautiful prayer mat I had ever seen for her, not that I had really seen many, but you get my gist. I just loved it, and I also loved the idea of it, it had a physical purpose, I loved the thought of laying this beautiful mat down to then do the purest thing. When he left, I asked Ayesha to show me, which she did. I remember thinking how wondrous, I want that in my life.

    She gently rolled it out and then proceeded to kneel on it, bowing forward and then coming back ever so slowly. I was mesmerised. To me it was as if you were honouring the prayer, not just praying, by the action, the whole display. It just flowed like it was the most natural thing in the world to do. While she prayed, I prayed that Ayesha would get better and live a life that was as beautiful as she was. Not one of us except Leanne had ever said anything about our prior life, not to my knowledge anyway. None of us ever asked one another about our reason for being there. It was almost like an unspoken rule, though probably it was more likely because not one of us had any room left in our minds for another thing. Leanne mentioned jumping off a bridge onto a motorway by way of explanation for all her scars, and if it hadn't been for that we probably wouldn't have known anything about her either. Well, prayers done, nearly time for bed, my yellow bedside lamp aglow and Horlicks at the ready.

Next morning, a new arrival. I was itching to get to know her. Maya was gutted, the rest in the main were not bothered either way. Tall, blonde and savvy, I thought, and I knew instinctively I would like her. Louise was her name, and she was as bubbly as you could get, I loved it. No messing around, she just jumped straight in, and her enthusiasm was infectious. I mean there obviously were still certain patients that even if you showed them the winning lottery ticket, they still would just have given that blank stare, the look of not happy or sad, maybe it's the meds? But us few that still had hope in our hearts and were not too dulled by the powerful drugs liked her instantly.

Like a long-lost pal, she took turns sitting chatting on our beds or in the day room, wherever it may be. My first conversation took a turn I wasn't expecting: she knew my son Blue. I frantically wanted to know everything she knew, like I did when anyone spoke of him. It was like a new wave on the shore, I would be awash with all the things I never knew. It made me feel closer to him in a way and I would desperately cling to that before the true reality set in, that in the fact I wouldn't be physically with him again until we were united in Heaven.

Louise loved him and I knew it wasn't that she just didn't want to say anything bad to a grieving mother. I know the above to be a fact. She described him to within an inch of his true personality! Funny, kind, thoughtful, pure and above all else she remembered the magical way he made everyone he met feel at ease, heard, loved and special. Yes, he took a wrong turn in the road, but that didn't make him a bad person. In fact, the only injustice inflicted was on himself and he paid the ultimate price. At that point I know he wasn't in control, the addiction was, albeit he was only an addict for three years. His funeral was testament to how loved he was, the hundreds that were there to say their goodbyes. Further testament to him, whenever speaking to even someone who had only just crossed paths with him momentarily, remember his presence still to this day. I am proud to say he is my son, and I will wait patiently to be with him again. In the meantime, these conversations with people, friends or family, will keep me steady on my road of trepidation, when I get scared, which is often and when it's unbearably overwhelming to think I have to live the rest of my life through without him. I also try to take comfort from the thought of him being with my parents, loved ones long gone and of course God.

Louise ended up as my new cigarette buddy. The only downside to that was I missed my chats with Mary. Sometimes when Louise engaged in conversations with others I would go over and talk with Mary, but it wasn't the same. Even though I loved Louise's crack Mary was a one-to one and I was well aware that the chats I had with her were the only ones she had, plus she intrigued me. The only place I ever spoke to Mary was downstairs outside while smoking; upstairs was strictly out of bounds which I respected and stuck by.

In the meantime, Louise didn't show, or should I say didn't care about gentle intrusion, which was good because it pushed certain patients to chat and engage, other than doing their usual loitering about mute. I was like her, but Louise was fresh blood and funny, so her humour opened little doors, in the patients' minds that is. We decided early on to make a point of herding them into the favoured day room, which was the large one at the bottom of the unit, a minimum once a day. Like a script off the doctor, or you know, a spoonful of sugar (Mary Poppins), we would make them all laugh if it killed us and stir reactions up like no drug can ever do. It was a very positive activity, I thought, whether they did too or not is another matter!

Our first mission wasn't really that successful, but God loves a trier as they say, so we just kept plugging away. Bit like my day job, we would have a small handover on my bed beforehand and talk tactics, like who would say what first etc, hilarious really when you think about it as we were patients ourselves. Have you ever seen *One Flew Over the Cuckoo's Nest* with Jack Nicholson? Brilliant film. Well, whoever wrote that must have had inside knowledge. Speaking for myself – though I think Louise would probably agree – I felt like his actions in the film were similar to what we did. We didn't have to worry about some of the things he had to though, like the fact they were all mega overly drugged, so much so he felt he needed to make an escape plan. After all the film was in the seventies or something, so that was probably true. Just the fact that the patients needed a laugh, it was good for them to find their voices and it was hugely important for them to engage in a group form and regain their lost confidence.

Jack Nicholson did not have the copious layers of false tan thank goddess, but we did have one thing in common and that was the scary hair. There was a fine line however between the fact that patients on one hand trusted each other, because after all we were in the same boat, and then on the other being wary because of paranoia, and this was probably because we all had a deeper understanding of how frigged up each of us all were and a kick-off could be triggered in a blink of an eye in so many ways. So, it was integral to our success that we were ready to step in should any grey areas be in danger of being breached and to cease fire and abort the mission if necessary.

That day's handover was to enter the room like it was random and then me and her to converse and tell a few funny stories about ourselves outside of the unit – that was key – and then to ask if any of them had a funny story about themselves. All of this would be done without removing their finger- or toenails or any waterboarding, I hoped. Yes, at times it was like pulling teeth, but nobody could curb our enthusiasm. A couple of them caved in, which was a good result. They weren't daft though, they started to suss our repetitive behaviour after a few days had passed. We would just have to come up with another favourable plan. It is unbelievably hard to keep a mentally unwell person engaged and with some it's downright impossible, so any small goal met was ginormous really!

Another girl arrived, Simone. She looked normal, and I was sure it was a huge mistake. Louise made her welcome straight away and then I followed suit. Same thing, no one knew why she was there, and no one would ever ask either. She was nice, quiet but nice, saying that next to me and Louise anyone was quiet.

When it came to the first time I was in the queue at the drugs cupboard with Louise I was blown away, as she knew every drug, every dosage and their intended purpose. To set the scene the drugs cupboard/room door would be open, the nurse inside of the room, shelves stocked with all things not controlled, locked cupboards stocked with all controlled drugs and the patients, i.e. myself, would be in a queue one behind another. So, you saw and heard everything that was said or given – if you were interested, that is. In the main nobody was, I think they just wanted their meds and that was that. But not Louise!

I was totally flabbergasted by her knowledge, I was like, ", you could be a bloody doctor!" Joking aside, she had to be clever to retain all that information, of that there was no doubt in my mind. When it was her turn with the nurse, some of her meds were wrong. Well she soon put that right, she rhymed off everything that should have been on her script including dosage and why she was on them. I don't know who was more shocked, me or the nurse! Hence to say she ended up getting the lot, ha!

Back in my room I asked her about my meds, me not remembering most of the names and her with her photographic memory, only going off what she witnessed at the drugs cupboard, as you get given them in a little pot, all while the nurses is relaying what they are at a spitfire rate. She informed me that most of them were antipsychotic meds and that if I didn't feel a hundred percent myself that was probably why as they had that dulling effect for obvious reasons. It was good to have a friend like this, I thought!

Nearing the latter half of my stay there I got some awful news: my friend's nephew had died. It was a terrible shock. I had known him all my life and both his parents as well, and they became all I could think about, the heartache they were now going through. I was determined that I wanted to go to his funeral. When I approached the nurses' station to ask if that was even a possibility, I really thought that there wouldn't be, but to my amazement they said yes, absolutely. When I told my family that I could attend, I think they were shocked by it too. They tried all ways to talk me out of it and they were partly right, because I had just ended up sectioned after my own son's funeral which was just weeks ago. But my recall was warped at that present time, my recollection of Blue was also fleeting, however bad that sounds. The brain protects itself in those terrible times. It's clever, as while you're in a state of shock – my shocked state lasted nearly a year – it blocks out all of the most unbearable things. With one pitfall though you're lucky to even be able to do the most menial tasks because it affects your concentration big time! I wasn't aware until looking back how much your concentration comes into play, i.e. even watching the TV, when I was able that is, I would have the volume full blast, thinking it was my hearing when in reality it was my inability to concentrate, and reading which I loved was definitely off the table.

The one thing I was sure of was what I was going to wear. I believed and still do as a mark of respect that you should be as smart as possible. So, I wanted my black trousers, white shirt and my red Gucci shoes brought in. Robert's dilemma was which ones, as I had copious pairs of black trousers and white shirts. I thought I won't push my luck and ask him to bring the lot in, he would be like Alice's husband with a big holdall, so I asked instead for a few of each, the ones that he thought would fit me.

My sister and brother-in-law were going with me as they also had known him and his family like me all their lives. He had a lovely send-off, it was just heartbreaking to see his parents and family grieving. At the wake I didn't want to get excitable, as I have that tendency when there's lots of people, even under normal circumstances, not meaning any disrespect whatsoever to anyone ever. It's just a trait that I have, maybe part of my later diagnosis. I chose to stay seated at all costs, not even to go to the bathroom if I could help it! That way I could avoid looking totally inappropriate and offending people that don't understand my behaviour, which I totally get, it's not that I don't know, that's why I had a plan. Even unwell I had some rationality.

Back at the Tranwell I felt like I was vindicated in the fact that I had always known there was nothing wrong with me and the proof was now in the pudding. Me attending the funeral and from my behaviour point of view, which was all appropriate and intact, said it all. If these lot didn't realise it, well, that was for them to live with not me. Even then though I had no thoughts of leaving or getting released, it just never ever crossed my mind. Maybe it was a stretch, for me I mean. I don't think my mind was capable of thinking very far ahead and I never once after my little solitary confinement spell had any feelings or inklings of home.

Leanne was the first to leave while I was there. I was deeply saddened by this, I loved Leanne, she was just so laid back and normal. Louise came up with the idea of a leaving gift, and me, Simone, Michaela and a few others gave money. We ended up with a canny amount in the kitty, which was great, and Louise's daughter got the gifts and a card for us.

INTO THE BLUE

We all went to her room as she was packing up and gave her her gifts, pjs, smellies etc. She was over the moon and couldn't thank us enough, she even had a few tears. There was a funny atmosphere I thought when she left, like a piece of the jigsaw was missing, I just wanted it to stay us forever.

We definitely had a camaraderie otherwise we wouldn't have all felt the way we did. I then had a new despair: before her departure the concept of anyone leaving was nil and void, but now I knew it to be true, I knew there would be others, and the dread filled me. My mind went to who would be next etc, as if we were going to the chopping block. Well, I had to stop those thoughts and put them out of my mind as quickly as they came in. I just couldn't go there so I would move on and put them to one side, for now.

Myself, Louise and Simone were sitting chatting in the small day room talking about what we were going to do that evening. We came up with a movie night. Great, I would get Robert to bring the popcorn in, Simone said she would get her hubby or mam, whoever was coming in on the visit, to bring the sweets and Louise would get her lot to bring some fizzy pop. Like jail probably, I've never been there myself, but I can guess it's the little things that get you by. It would certainly help us with getting over the fact that Leanne had left.

So here we were like the three amigos for movie night, treats at the ready and a pile of old, very old, DVDs to go through. We poured the pop, opened the sweets, talked, Louise making us laugh. It was good to see Simone laughing as she had looked sad since her arrival, even under her smile. To be honest the DVDs were crap, probably donated or something. We hummed and hawed over them but ended up just telling each other stories, which were probably a lot more interesting anyway.

I told them about when I ordered all the Givenchy stuff, after my man died, sixteen grands' worth to be exact, which included a baby pink cropped bomber jacket that has still never seen the light of day. Also, the time I ordered a pair of Vetements green glittery sock boots that had a lighter as a heel with My Little Pony on. The only website I could get them from, as they had sold out everywhere (see, I do have good taste), was a Russian website. Desperate to get them, as everything is imminent with me, some days more so than others, I really didn't trust the Russians but what the frig! What's one thousand six hundred pounds between foes? It really was like 'Russian roulette' in my mind, a roll of a dice to whether I received them or not, it was nail-biting stuff. I think I've learnt to thrive on living on a knife edge through all the ordering I've done throughout the years.

But the day of their arrival was like 'the parting of the seas', not only a miracle but a moment of historical value! I now trusted the Russians, even bloody Putin – well maybe not him – but the rest of them defo! Who knew! Even the United Nations couldn't make a U-turn that quick. One click, in the cart, money given, on the plane, out for delivery, delivered and that was that they were no longer my foes but my allies. HURRAY!

Louise and Simone couldn't get over it, the money I had spent, the things I had bought, the whole shooting match. Little did they know I had loads more of those stories – well, a humongous closet full of them to be exact. We laughed and laughed. It was a good night had by all.

INTO THE BLUE

I woke up with an idea of being proactive, so the plan was to hike every morning and every afternoon! Where? I thought, well I didn't have many options really, in fact I only had one, the car park outside, that was fine it would do the trick. So, leisure gear on after my morning bath and ear pods in, music chosen, I was away. Up the car park I march and then back down in a full circle, then repeat. I loved that, the freedom, the fresh air, my music. I still love walking now, I have always loved walking, and I probably will forever. My lovely dad used to walk the hind legs off me, when I was small. Maybe when I was like six or seven, I asked my mam for roller skates so I could keep up with him when we walked to my nana's house every Sunday. He walked that fast naturally and only had one speed; he didn't take into consideration that my little legs were half the size of his. I got the roller skates and like I thought I not only could keep up with him, but I could overtake him, amazing. So that's where I get it from.

That routine went on religiously for the rest of my stay. I did worry in the beginning that other patients might ask to join in, but they never did thank goodness. I wasn't being selfish, I just knew as soon as I started it, I needed this small amount of time on my own. So, my day started early. Not so much for some of the other patients, Maya still liked her lie-ins. She had been absent from my company as of late, I couldn't fix the fact that she could only do one to one. I wasn't willing to pay the price and nor did I want to put up with childlike behaviour, I thought.

The only others who kept similar hours to me in the morning were Viv, dressed to impress, only missing her briefcase or some very important documents, Alice and Liz.

They were like a couple of Siamese twins with their super-clean, super-starched, super-industrial steam-ironed clothes. I swear if they took them off, they would stand up by themselves and with not a hair on their head out of place. Mind you, although Alice's hair never budged, it did leave a lot to be desired. I think her hubby cut it. It made sense really, I could imagine Alice never got anywhere except places like this or the odd time home. Bless him, he did his utmost best that was clear, but his forte was clearly not in the hair department. It was obvious that he had just placed a bowl on her head and cut round it. She had really thick hair, like I mean inches thick, poker straight so you can picture it. Liz pre-Alice Ming Dynasty was put together, but daily she was morphing more and more into Alice. Similar non-descriptive clothing, definitely no bright colours, actually they were pushing the boat out at pastels. It was also clearly a running theme that the daily attire would be plain trousers and a round neck T-shirt, definitely no V-necks, even a high one, sometimes a plain blouse, no way on Heaven's earth with a pattern.

So there the four of us were in the morning, you couldn't have gotten more different if you had tried, what a motley crew.

The staff approached me and asked if I would like home visits. Well, I wasn't bothered but I was interested to see what they entailed. It was simple. I could go home for a few hours but then had to come back. I lived about a fifteen-minute walk away from the unit. Originally in the beginning they had asked me if I would rather be at a different unit because I worked there and people and staff would be around the grounds etc, for confidentiality, and of course I said no. I would have said no ordinarily anyway, but at that time I didn't even know why I was there, let alone be moved, though that was the whole time actually. The Tranwell unit was in the hospital grounds as in a separate building, it was part of the Newcastle Trust Hospitals, and the building was at the bottom of the Gateshead Trust's site. I rather liked it as staff would pass on their way to work and I would wave, and they even stopped for a chat if they had time, just shooting the breeze. Also, it meant I got more visits from my friends/colleagues from my unit. Who wanted to come to the hospital on a day off? It would be like a busman's holiday. So, it was a win win!

I told Robert that night of my new info, the home visits that is, and I'm not sure what he thought of that, his face said more stress! But maybe I had it wrong.

The next day, like a bolt of lightning in the car park on my morning walk, I thought well, I might as well pop along to Sue's, my sister's house, for a cuppa rather than go back inside for one. She lived one street from me, so it didn't take me long. I knocked on her door and when she opened it, I vividly remember the shock-horror on her face. I can remember thinking, well that's not very nice. I thought she would be ecstatic, yeah, she wouldn't have had time to get balloons and a banner or anything, but to have this reaction?

I eventually had to say, "Well, are you going to invite me in then?" as she stood with her mouth agape. Once in I said, "Stick the kettle on then," thinking maybe giving her prompts would be more beneficial as she looked like she was in a state of shock. She proceeded to put the kettle on. The only words that she could utter were "Do they know you have escaped?" I'm standing there in her kitchen thinking what the hell is she talking about?

I tried to reassure her, but we kept going around in circles for a while, until she eventually accepted that I was on what you call a home visit, and how legit it was. Although I'm still not entirely sure the latter was true, as I had not gone back onto the unit to inform them. Sue told me later as soon as I had left, she rang Robert and the smoke signals followed, Sue being 'Full of Worry' head squaw and Robert Chief 'I'll Follow Suit'. Neither of them wanted to squeak on me so they decided the best course of action was to just give me enough time to get back and then Robert would ring my mobile, like he was just wanting to chat with me or something. It worked, I was back safe and sound all present and correct.

Chapter seven
Breakfast and home leave

It's funny how the unit really was the centre of my universe. There are only a few times in my life that I've felt the concept of that phrase, and this was one of them. Outside of it wasn't really my concern, nor did I have any inclination for it to be either. To be honest that's why that place really did what it said on the tin for me! I needed minimal stimulation and none of the worries that come with day-to-day life. No matter how much you try to shield a person at home they will always come into play, it is an impossible task. Inside a unit, in the main you just eat, sleep, repeat with a sprinkle of activities thrown in.

Everyone had the same rooms, same facilities and speaking for myself everyone had some level of understanding, albeit to different degrees, that we were all unwell in some way. Not that I think it was at the forefront of our minds but somewhere deep inside it was. That subconscious thought was the building block of our comradeship, like the foundations of a house, you forget that it's there, but every house needs it! Yeah, I'm not saying that you wouldn't get any kick-offs, but we needed that undercurrent, a flowing stream, constantly keeping things moving, exactly the way a body of water needs it.

This was an aspect of hospitals that I had not much, if any, knowledge of. When I look back at it, where I was certainly had it down to a fine art. The staff, the same ones I thought got paid for nothing, ha! Fit like a hand in a glove. They were always meant to do just that, the blending into the background, the non-judgement, no contradiction, no conditions, no opinions either way, there if you needed them but quiet and nonintrusive otherwise.

How strange we must have all looked. I've often thought; if you could have had a peek, taken the roof of the building and peered in, like a doll's house only with moving parts, and just watched the comings and goings. I do know there will be some bad facilities as it's all par for the course sadly, but for me I will continue to speak about my experience with total optimism and will forever be grateful for it.

As for how unwell I was when I went in, of course the drugs helped, but I know the whole set-up and principles were what helped me immensely. I just wish that places like that could be a gold standard for the not so good ones. But on the whole the NHS isn't very good at that, they talk a lot about it, meetings after meetings all senior management, on God knows how much an hour and they continue to get it wrong. Anyway, enough about that, it doesn't take much to get me started about all that and I've got more pressing things to talk about!

I would love to meet all the patients again who were there when I was, firstly to see how they are doing now and secondly to see how they felt about their time there. This is not meant in any way derogatory but sadly I think a good percentage of them probably would have had numerous admissions since, whether it be there or another psychiatric facility.

Time for breakfast club, and Maya and I could barely contain our excitement at the prospect of having our eggs benedict. Sounds posh, but maybe it was like a last supper on death row sort of thing going on, as you ordered prior, stating exactly what you would like, and they got it in. It was the reverse when you think of it – instead of getting your last meal before your stay there or anywhere else was terminated, we were getting it and then being kicked out! Set free!

Maya was designated cook, and I was the washer-upper, great for me as let's just say cooking isn't one of my talents. Myself and Robert's duties are dished out the same at home as above. She couldn't wait to show off her cooking skills and I was hoping and praying that the food would live up to the expectations that were going on in my mind. Bar the odd Cornish pasty I had lived on sushi while being there so you can understand the magnitude of it in my mind.

We went down to the kitchen, Maya reassuring me constantly about how phenomenal it was going to be. Up to this point in my life I had never eaten eggs benedict before. I'm not sure why because I had always thought it sounded lush. I set the knives and forks out on the table like the good little housewife I was and stuck the kettle on for our cuppa while she got cracking. I sat with bated breath and bathed in all the lovely aromas going on in the room, my tastebuds waiting patiently.

I'll give her her due, she cooked with a confidence that made me pretty sure it was going to be good. The moment had arrived. Beaming from ear to ear, she placed our plates down on the table. Wow was all I could think. A male member of staff who was in the kitchen with us even looked shocked, in a good way.

We all got stuck in as she had made him a plate too. It lived up to it all and some, it was faultless. I remember thinking, how many bloody talents has this woman got? I probably told her that too. I savoured the last morsel like I was in my cell and living with the thought that I was never going to taste food ever again! I washed up and cleaned down the cooker and benches all the while thinking, why is she here when she could be doing so many amazing things? Maybe all the amazing things simply stopped filling her up. It's something I'll sadly never know. The more time I spent with her, her character became even more complicated and complex to me. Her personality was like a beautiful intricate web, and she was the spider. So only she knew the wondrous patterns that were made, where they started and where they finished.

Over the next week or so I popped home a couple of times. It was always right after my walk around the car park, and yes, I did inform my nurse those times. Robert was at work in the day so I would just go to my sisters for a cuppa and a chat. When I was ready, I would just make my way back to the place I was now calling home. The crazy bit is I never once thought I'll just pop in at my house as Sue had a key. I don't know how it came about as I can't remember but I was going home to stay overnight. I would love to tell you how it was, but I have no recall whatsoever, other than it happened. I don't know if it's a thing or not, but I think it's funny that it was my house, the same house where the policeman had informed me that Blue had died, the same house which had been Blue's home, the house where real life happened, who knows?

The huge problem that I can remember was I arrived back to the unit the next morning only to find my bedroom was gone, no longer mine, it had someone else in it and all of my belongings had been bagged up! My memory seemed to switch off when I arrived home and switch back on the minute I landed back on the unit.

Well, let the meltdown begin! Devastated was an understatement of how I felt, I didn't know if I was going to vomit, cry, have hysterics or do all three! But my inability to multitask at the time saved me and everyone else from having to go through all the shenanigans that they had all been through when I first arrived on the unit and ended up in solitary confinement. Instead, I stood in the corridor like a lost soul with no vocabulary whatsoever.

Bless her, Marie, who was one of the quietest ones, the girl with the anorexia nervosa, came to my rescue and offered her room to me, or at least to share for now. I think that she had been through it herself a few times. She helped carry my bags to her room. I was pissed that the staff didn't seem to think that this was an ordeal for me. Looking back though they may have had a couple of reasons for doing so. One would be this was just a bed availability issue and that it was a regular occurrence; two, they played it down like you would to a child who was on the brink of kicking off, AKA reverse psychology. None of those helped me though.

There was me and Marie sitting on her age seven quilt cover, me too numb to speak and her trying to make everything alright.

My phone went and it was Robert to see if I was settled and sorted. SETTLED!!!!!!!! He couldn't have picked a worse word to say to me. I found my voice and vocabulary no problem then. A tirade came of all the things I was feeling and had felt since I knew my room was gone, which by the way felt like a week ago when in reality it had been a couple of hours max. I went into the bathroom so I could cry and scream down the phone to him. I begged him to sort it out and through tears told him that even though Marie was lovely, I didn't know how much longer I could sit in her room. Poor Robert! In his mind I had gone right back to the beginning, and he thought that this was it, this was how it was going to be from now on in.

He did in fact ring the unit. He had no idea about hospital protocols, he also assumed that my bed, my cosy lovely room, would just be waiting for me when I got back. How he was able to do all this while working in a mega stressful job on his busy site at the time I don't know. The staff informed him that this was normal practice and that someone was leaving later that day and that then would be my new room. So, he probably had to take ten Valium (joke) before ringing me back to give me the good news. What he probably didn't expect was my reaction, a whole other tsunami of a meltdown came. Another room! That was no good, did they not know that only my original room would do? I told him that they would have to do a three-way room swap or something, otherwise I would gladly get myself put back in solitary confinement.

Now I was privy to Ayesha's behaviour and how she must have felt. You know, the Muslim girl with the beautiful eyes who I took into my room and had to give a cigarette to in order to calm her down after the very same thing happened to her. I thought she was a spoiled brat at the time, well I was now in her shoes and it was nothing to do with karma and everything to do with the state of our minds.

I can remember feeling violated. Even if they had given my room back to me that instant, it could never be the same. My lovely pictures couldn't be put up on the wall the same as before, my dressing table, the layout, nothing was ever going to be the same as it had been.

Marie tried all ways to help the situation, but now I had found my voice she could barely get a word in edgewise. I think they may have nearly had to find a bed for Robert that night, never mind me, as when he came in he looked like he could do with a long lie down in a dark room for a couple of days.

Eventually my new room was free. I took my stuff in reluctantly. FFS, I was further down the corridor now. My beautiful bathroom was no longer across from me, instead I had the shitty tiny shower room next to me that no one used, with barely enough room to swing a cat in. My nerves were in shreds and at the time I thought I had no hope of recovering from the day's events.

I took some of my things out of the bags but not everything, I thought it was like a protest, I would show them! What they had done to me that day was my only train of thought. No pictures were going up on the wall, no clothes in the wardrobe, this was my only defence, my only way of showing everyone how utterly cruel it had all been. Those feelings were as real as real could be in my mind at the time – the intensity of it, no kidding, was similar to that of a prisoner sitting on death row who is innocent. Just to give you a scale, a correct comparison of the enormity, I know that's a lot and may seem slightly overboard but it's true.

A few days later, behind the scenes my consultant psychiatrist, the very nice Sem, had asked Robert to come in to see him, unbeknownst to me. He wanted to know if Robert thought I was ready for home. Robert told a little white lie, or maybe a little larger, that yes indeed he thought I was ready. In fact, Robert just didn't want me getting too comfortable and familiar in a place like that, he even hated and questioned every time I asked for more clothes or other items brought in. His reactions always puzzled me at the time as I never knew he felt that way. Robert went on to ask if a trip would be good for me, as we had one booked at the end of the next month. My consultant asked where. Robert told him it was Amsterdam and then to see André Rieu in concert at Maastricht. He said certainly not! He said it would be far too busy, especially because it was summertime, and the concert was a definite no go. He followed it up by saying the polar opposite was what I needed, no stimulation, i.e. people, busy places, noise, chat, shops the list went on.

I can remember much later at home Robert told me about it, the conversation, everything, and I thought what a traitor that consultant was, after all he was friggin Dutch, he should have been jumping five-bar gates that I loved André Rieu! But it just goes to show how even at home after the Tranwell I was still poorly as I never ever asked about the holiday because I didn't even remember we were going.

Back on the unit I gave myself a shake and tried to get back into the groove. I don't think things were ever the same for me, but my natural personality tried hard to shine through the room situation. What else helped me was the poor young girl, the new admission, who was now in my room. It was a few days before anybody even got a glimpse of her as she never left the room, 'my room'. She must have been desperate to see staff, so she had to venture out to go to the nurses' station, another little ploy that worked a treat! She looked very young, long hair, a fringe the same length which covered her whole face, intentional I thought, black clothes from head to toe, coat and trainers on like she was ready to go at any given moment. Now you need to understand the unit was like a sweatbox, it was like being in the Sahara Desert only with water, the windows did not open as they were fixed shut. It's a wonder we didn't all walk around in our underwear, and she had all these layers on like she was about to summit Everest! I'm sure the phenomenal heat was to aid the process of knocking us out at night, the only trouble was then that it carried into the next day.

I gently tapped on her door when she had not come out again. I did hesitate in case it was an invasion of her space, but then I rejected that as, one, this was my room originally and two, she was far too young to be in a place like this, never mind holed up in her room. I had to knock a few times, probably much to her dismay, but eventually she answered. Her long fringe preceded her and if she leant any further forward towards the floor, I would have thought she was bowing to me. I introduced myself and told her that I had been in this same room when I first came in and that it had been nice when people came to my door and spoke to me, albeit hers had been shut and mine was always open but that was just a misdemeanour.

It's so hard when there is no eye contact. It's very strange, I thought, I don't know how far I will get with Cousin IT, but I'll give it my best shot. When she spoke, it was mainly a mumble and the decibel reading must have been zero, but I managed to hear that her name was Genene, though only after asking her to repeat it numerous times. I gave her a whole backstory of me having ear problems as a child and grommet operations etc, etc, laying it on with a trowel to get some small nugget of information. Then that was that, the end of our amazing conversation. She said, "I'll have to go," and I can remember thinking 'Where are you going? Narnia? Maybe through your doorless wardrobe, can I come?'

Until the day I left the unit I only knew a couple of things about her: she liked to draw and colour in, and she also liked to self-harm. Although she tried very hard to hide it, you could see the marks on her lower wrists and hands. Now I hoped to God that they weren't that low down because she had run out of room higher up. Or maybe she simply wanted someone, anyone to notice and therefore see the pain that was going on inside of her.

I felt really bad about her, in fact she bothered me more than anyone else. Yeah, you had Maya who could be reclusive, but this was different. Her sadness oozed out from her with such force that it seemed to penetrate through the walls of her room, and through her forever-closed door. I hated passing her room when I went for a cigarette or to the drugs cupboard because I could physically feel it and like a black cloud it engulfed my whole being.

Plus, something else that unsettled me was the fact that I wholeheartedly knew that this tiny thing was unfixable and she would continue her life as a tortured soul. Her mind was as blackened as the clothes she wore, and her black hair was like the Iron Curtain with a steel-like determination that no person or thing could ever penetrate.

Over the coming days myself, Louise, Simone and Marie just did the rounds in each of our rooms, yes, my shitty one and the small day room of course. It's funny isn't it that a certain portion of us favoured the small day room and the other half the large day room. It's like we put our mark on it and that was that. Now and again, I would venture into the large day room to check on Alice, but to be honest I lost the will, and I didn't feel the need of prolonging the agony. She was never going to be good either, my heart couldn't take the concept of it. How her hubby or family felt about it, God only knows!

Because of my need for a deeper understanding and a desire for them to be a fully healed human beings, my judgement was clouded to such an extent that I couldn't think in a clinical fashion about them or their situation. I've always been a glass half full person, my excellent GP Dr Ward said I was high functioning, so it was all so alien to me. I take my hat off to all the people trying to help them, it's a complicated and I bet frustrating and thankless task in the main. Then to boot, how can you define 'helping' when the person in front of you cannot be fixed, never mind wanting to be helped? It all blows my mind and is definitely up there on the sad front.

Louise never stopped being friendly and up for a laugh, Simone was lovely but more reserved than us. Lousie told me all the stories of her times at raves and Blue being there and how the MCs always gave him a shout-out as he knew everyone in the room. Still to this day his friends send me videos of the shout-outs! He still gets them now. I used to worry about his partying ways, like most mothers do, but now I'm pleased that he lived life to the full and had all the fun and the laughs that went with it along the way. Louise said she loved him as everyone else did and that no one ever had a bad word to say about him and to this present day, not saying it because he's mine but I've never met anyone who just hasn't had anything but love for him.

I don't know how, but Louise found out that Simone was admitted after being date-drugged and raped by a couple of men. It was heartbreak city in that place. I'm pleased in a way I wasn't well myself because to take all these tortured souls on board a hundred percent would have been terrible.

We pretended to be drinking the hard stuff when we congregated in my room. I made my speciality drink which was one-part diluted orange juice and two parts Schweppes tonic. Then I'd put the tunes on, requests of course, and we just made our own fun. I did wish I could reverse what Louise told me about Simone, but I couldn't, so what was done was done, I just tried my best to behave in a normal manner around her.

Robert told me later that he had been asked to go to the unit a few times to discuss my past and present behaviours. My consultant had asked him what I had been like before my admission. Had I had feelings of grandeur? Had I acted upon them? Had I been fast and unable to concentrate? He said yes to all of the above. The consultant told him that he had diagnosed me with Mania Bipolar, Bipolar 1, and that I would have had it all of my life, but it had been magnified and brought to the forefront with Blue's death. He informed Robert that on my discharge my care would be taken over by the Community Mental Team and that I would have my own CPN and see a psychiatrist at the Dryden Road facility, also I would continue with my anti-psychotic drugs. I think Robert would have just been relieved to know that he didn't have to carry the whole burden of me by himself, I know I would! I can't remember them ever giving me the diagnosis while I was there. If they did my memory hid it from me, or maybe it wasn't appropriate with my mental state.

INTO THE BLUE

So, I'm swanning around in there free from any idea of anything else that was going on. To be frank I had no idea of time, dates, months so I don't know how much good it would have done anyway. I mean we can all laugh about it now, even though it was quite serious at the time. But I always like to find the silver linings in everything that happens. One of my silver linings of that time, because there are a few, is that I may have never got diagnosed and my family, especially Robert, would have never got to see how serious Bipolar was and can be. If they had learnt about it any other way, they may not have had any foresight into how dangerous it can be and all the signs to look out for when an episode is starting or has started.

It must have been an unbelievably hard time for my family, the great loss of Blue and then me in there. My poor beautiful dad, he was already heartbroken over his grandson, who really was like his son. Blue's dad stopped seeing him when he was five years old, so my dad stepped in. Well, my mam and dad were both amazing support to me and Blue. How my dad coped I just do not know. My mam had died only a couple of years prior, and he was still in the midst of that grief. He never came to the Tranwell to see me, I don't really know why, but I'm guessing it was all too much for him and after all he was eighty-four at the time. I mean, to see your child sectioned and in a mental health institute, you might as well say you've just lost another child, how much can one person take on? If he or my family made that decision I'm pleased, pleased he did not see me like that and in that case, ignorance really is bliss!

On the sunny days me and Louise would go down for a cigarette and sit on the bench and forget to go back inside. The men from their wing would come down in dribs and drabs.

There were a few of them that knew Blue, after all he was a huge personality and Gateshead is quite small. They would tell me their stories of him, and I loved it, I'll never tire of that ever. The crack was great, cause in the beginning, I was more than happy with my own little contained ship, but this was opening new doors for me, and I was really enjoying lots of different company again.

As I told you before, there wasn't much Louise didn't know about medication, so here she was again asking how many milligrams this, how many milligrams that? I was flabbergasted by it all, and secretly liked the fact that she was telling the blokes what to do. You could tell they were all startled by her knowledge. Some days she had a friggin queue going on, this one wanted to know if this was right and that one wanted to know if his dosage was correct or enough etc.

I told her, I said, "Louise, you've missed your vocation!" and the very next thing I said was "Have you got a criminal record?" for her DBS that is for a job in the health care profession, I love but I was thinking laterally! Cut me some slack!

Simone never came out. She didn't smoke, but didn't even go for fresh air. I'm pleased though as it could have been an awful situation with the men being there. There were only three of us that smoked, me, Louise and Mary. I did start playing my tunes again for Mary in between all the other stuff, as much jazz as I could find. Never knew if she appreciated it or not, I like to think she did.

We pestered Genene at intervals, and I had an idea to ask her about her colouring in to sway her to open up slightly. There was progress, I managed to be able to sit on the edge of her bed and look through some of her books for about ten to fifteen minutes tops. I think the man who climbed in our Queen Elizabeth's window at Buckingham Palace and then got into her bedroom while she slept, then proceeded to sit on her bed and chat to her when she woke had more luck than I did. He had the whole of the British constabulary and Secret Service after him. Just saying!

The minuscule amount of time I sat with her, all I could think was she must be sweating with all that get up on, coat and all. The germs going on under that attire only a sheep dip could sort out. I'm not trying to be humiliating about it, just she never bathed, that I know for sure. Maybe she simply froze at the prospect of even stripping off behind a closed door, or she never trusted that the home-made signs we would stick on the door when it was taken would keep anyone from coming in. There were no locks on any of the doors we used for obvious reasons – another example of being a prisoner of our own minds. I think everyone is on a small scale, a little is good if it is in the name of fear, but this was on a level that if you didn't witness it, it's hard to understand or even believe.

The time had come! I was told that I would be leaving at the end of the week. I can remember thinking, 'where did that come from?' I knew full well that people had left while I was there but honestly, I was always in the frame of mind of 'that will never happen to me'. I never thought about it prior, nor did I ever think 'is it me next?' I just thought I was part of the fixtures and fittings.

So, when it came it was almost like I didn't know what it meant. Looking back maybe my mind just couldn't or wouldn't go there, back to the reality of life and the life without my son in it.

That's the only thing with places like that, you're not living in reality, it's a little cocoon, a cloud that envelops you and protects you from all the bad weather of the outside world. Yet the exact same thing that helps you get better, a calm unstimulated environment with none of the worries of ordinary day to day life, then smacks you in the face like an atomic blast when it's time for home. The false reality that you never even knew you were living in is pulled from under your feet like a 'gigantic genie and the lamp' magic carpet.

I showed face of course in front of all my friends/patients when they arrived one by one at my room to give their condolences. I felt like Marlon Brando in the movie *The Godfather*, when they would come to show him their respect. Not that they kissed the ring or anything, I didn't have one on! But it did feel epic, ha! I think the way all our minds were at the time and our hearts, that feeling of a unity that only a place like that can give, if you want it, was why our very own cooperation, was shattered every time there was a discharge. Like a huge jigsaw, pieces would go missing and even though you tried to rebuild it, it would never be the same as it was. So, I decided the best course of action was deny, deny, deny, to myself that is. It works for all the governments and congressmen and women of the world so why shouldn't it work for me? As Winston Churchill said (I did like his speeches),' "Success consists of going from failure to failure without loss of enthusiasm." So I would 'fight on the beaches and on the land' because I would 'Never Give In'! My little handover to myself consisted of all the above and behaving as normal as possible. Yes, I thought, that would do the trick. They are playing games with my emotions, so I'll beat them at their own game! I filled my mind with the whole concept of what they were doing to me rather than what was happening, as the latter was too inconceivable for my mind to take on board.

The next few days are slightly blurry for me, but I do know there was a lot of chat, humour and kindness. Louise as always chivvied everyone along and she did a grand job, Alice participated which was woza to me, hence Liz did too, and I will always appreciate the love from everyone there. They did it even though it was their darkest hour too, which is something else! I never spoke to Robert about going home and he knows me well enough to know to just go with it. If I don't talk about something it's because it's too hard or nigh on impossible for me to do so, it's that simple.

This here is a prime example of the above, that unspoken rule between me and Robert. I never knew Dr Ward, my GP, was retiring until the day I needed him again (this was a couple of years after the Tranwell). I rang the surgery for an appointment only to have a young male receptionist inform me of the news. I was devastated – he may as well have died. When Robert rang me later that day to see if I had been able to get an appointment, I quickly told him through choked tears what had happened and then I followed it up with "I can't speak about it again for now," which he knew meant a while. He had a more in depth understanding than most how impossible it was for me and that I was also trying to protecting my mind in doing so. I mourned him, I mourned the fact that I had lost a doctor who knew almost without words what was wrong. I had gone through it all with him, first my mam's death, then Blue's, then needing to be sectioned, then my dad's death and later living with Bipolar, my new diagnosis. It takes time to build up trust with people never mind a GP, so when you have it, I'm telling you cherish it. But he was one of a kind. I'm a hard person to handle on a good day, never mind a bad one and handle me he did! I followed everything he said to the latter. When you're dealing with someone like me, or someone with any mental health, diagnosed or undiagnosed, it is integral to everything from the get-go to have that trust. Also respect, in order to be able to say all the mad things you're feeling and then to be able to listen and take lead from him or her. The heightened feelings of paranoia are enough to put you off even making the bloody appointment in the first place and if then the GP makes one wrong move, well! That's you not going to the doctors in a hurry again. I know that's one fine tightrope for the GP, but that's just the way mental health is. I always thought that he was Heaven-sent to me, like literally! He was the right amount of firm but fair, kind and empathetic, his clever silences made you talk more than you wanted to, but when he talked you listened. I heard he was an ex-major in the British Army and that's exactly 'what the doctor ordered' ha, in my many times of need. But more on that later.

The day had come, and it was not only a surreal feeling but also a confusing one for my mind. Louise, Marie, and Simone came to my room with my gifts and cards. I opened them like you do on a Christmas morning or your birthday, only it wasn't a celebration for me. Although very thoughtful and super sweet I couldn't muster up the enthusiasm that they all deserved. Smellies, pjs, a beautiful teardrop necklace which I'll keep forever. I loved them and I was really grateful but my sadness I couldn't hide.

Me and Louise went out for numerous cigarettes. I know she is clever enough to have known my deeper feelings but bless her, the troper she is, she hid it with humour and endless chat, and I really appreciated that. One last conversation with Mary, I knew better than to talk about me leaving, no nonsense was my approach from the beginning to now the end. I'm not sure looking back if she knew I was going home, I'd like to think if she did, she might miss these chats, after all I was the only person she talked to, or at the very least she missed me putting her tunes on.

I made sure to go to Alice and Liz to say my goodbyes. I couldn't help it but I flustered Alice – much to her dismay, full arms around her body, a cuddle that she probably hadn't had in quite some time, well it was done now. Liz got the same, why not I thought, they could worry about it when I was gone.

The beautiful, complicated Maya came to see me. She gave me some of her artwork that she had drawn especially. I loved them all. Not many words were exchanged. I think we conveyed our thoughts by just sitting next to one another. Maybe it was just too hard for us both, maybe no words would have sufficed.

Ayesha wasn't there that day as she was on another home visit. Viv was the only patient I never said bye to. Well, not a word had passed between us the whole time, why push the boat out now? I thanked all the staff for taking care of me and told them I would inform anyone who asked how brill they all were!

Robert came in the afternoon for me. I was all packed up. I gave my lovely yellow lamp and teddy to Louise, she deserved it, she should have been on the payroll for all of her hard work in jollying everyone along. I thought it was appropriate that they stay anyway, a little bit of me when I had gone.

Just like that, all the stuff put in the boot of the car, one last tab with Louise and away I went. All I could think was, I wish I was Louise. You know when you were younger and you made friends on holiday, when it was time to say goodbye to them to go to the airport and the sun is shining and people are splashing around in the pool? Well, it was a bit like that.

Chapter eight
Home

That feeling carried on when I walked in the house, putting my bags in instead of my suitcase, no sun-kissed tan to be seen on my body, but the exact same feeling on my mind. There was nothing else for it, I started unpacking. I've always had that ability no matter what's occurring in my life. I know as long as I'm doing! As in 'the verb', any kind of action, as long as I'm moving forward that will get me through somehow.

My mind still wasn't well enough to go as far cleaning the house, but I was able to tidy little things or put things away. Robert treated me with not only kid gloves but silk ones during this period. God only knows how scary it must have been for him, I love him for that, and it changed our relationship forever moving forward. That level of trust can only occur in certain situations. The Jewish religion believes when helping to choose a spouse for their children the main thing is that they are picking someone who can replace the parents. I love that train of thought. I am testament to that and anyone in my predicament or similar would not only need that to happen but would welcome it. Robert was not only my partner, but he also then became a parent to me as well in our relationship. The extra level of trust I was talking about before is what I'm describing now, the type of trust you unequivocally have from the day you're born with your parents is what I now had with him. That's what they mean by it and when at some point in your life when your parents are gone that trust is needed moving forward and you are joined with a bond that is not love but a trust and a respect that allows you to follow each other through life when one or the other is lost. It's a beautiful thing when it happens, and I do appreciate that not everyone will have a chance to know it. I never knew that that was the direction my relationship was going in for a good while never fully appreciating it because of my predicament. I look back now, and I can see it all and how it came to be. I will always be thankful of it and see it for the wonderous thing it is.

One consolation, the weather was still lovely, so out into the garden I would go, in and out all day long. When I was sitting out there, I always played my music on my little speaker. Even though I didn't think of Blue's death or of him being dead, I would incessantly play his funeral songs. Robert gently spoke to me about it, saying that maybe it wasn't appropriate, to which I said I didn't understand and that I was going to play them regardless. He then asked if I could at least turn the volume down, which I did. I think subconsciously I was trying to unlock my feelings by playing them.

Prior to Blue's death I would call in at my parents' daily, take them both out twice a week, every single week. On top of that I would be on the phone with them easily two, three times a day. I was super close to them and that continued after my mam died. I would do the exact same routine with my dad. Not now. There wasn't one part of me that wanted to go to my dad's. I knew I had to, but the fear it instilled in me almost made me freeze when it came down to it. Robert at the finish had to strongly persuade me to go, he spent hours explaining why. It's hard for people to understand, I know that I'm saying although I couldn't contemplate Blue's death, I could acknowledge that was the reason I found it difficult when it came to my father. The only way I can explain it is that it was like a tiny window or box in my mind that allowed me to recognise no-go zones and I could equate the reasons and feelings of others just not my own. I would go down, but my heart never let me stay the way I used to. Looking at the great sadness in my dad's eyes, not only for Blue but for me, was too much for my soul to take on board. That in itself was a great burden for me to carry. I knew that my dad needed me, he needed my physical presence to put his mind at rest and I just couldn't give him what he wanted.

At some point I knew I had to help myself, I knew this was too huge and too difficult to just walk side by side with it. One day, a good few years earlier, I was at my mam and dad's, me and my mam on the sofa and my dad sat opposite in his armchair, and he said, "Claire, if we were to put our problems in a heap we would always pick our own back out." I said I had never heard that saying before, what did it mean? He said, "It means there is always someone worse off!" That saying came to my mind like a bolt of lightning. Like I said before, everything happens for a reason and I believe my dad said that to me so I could remember it when I needed to. I also unequivocally know now that things do happen for a reason, because there were a lot more situations like that.

That was it, I went straight on the internet and looked for books that were true accounts based on people who had been through difficult times or suffering. I bought the first books that more or less came straight up in the search, going with the 'meant to be' theme. There were three books about the Auschwitz concentration camps. The first book was by an author who became a tattooist in the camp who lost every member of his family, then later became a world-renowned psychiatrist. The second and third books were in the same vein, only by a female. She also lost all of her loved ones in Auschwitz and she too went on to become a world-renowned psychiatrist.

I started reading them as soon as they arrived. That was a task in itself as my concentration was shot, but I just kept going. I had a gut feeling these books were going to save me from myself! Somewhere deep inside I knew to keep my head above water I had to remind myself like my dad told me of people who were much worse off than myself. I always lived life knowing that but at this point in my life I needed that reminder with everything in my being. I got lost in those books but getting lost freed me from myself!

Between reading, on my tab breaks in the garden I started to ask God to help me. I told God that I didn't think I had the strength to keep going and so I asked Him to please give me the strength. I was then starting to feel the heartbreak and I literally thought I was going to die of a broke heart, it was a real physical pain. The above I would repeat throughout the days over the following weeks. There was no shining light or vision of God, but this certain day in the garden I repeated the same request, it was no different to all the other days. All I can tell you is that I felt it, I felt His presence in my very soul, I knew He was with me, I knew I was receiving the strength I had been asking for, I knew He knew I needed Him, and He was filling me up with all I asked for. This might not accord with everyone's beliefs, but I can only account for myself and relay my story to you. I'll will never forget it as long as I live and still even now thank Him for his presence when I needed Him the most and I will always be eternally grateful. I persist even now

INTO THE BLUE

to affirm that I need His strength sometimes. He gave it to me, that's all I can tell you. Even though that time was horrendous, I knew it was a beautiful wondrous thing that happened to me.

I started walking Bertie again, admiring the beauty of the world in front of me on our outings. I was walking for my son and looking at all the things he could no longer see in this world. Yes, I was starting slowly to think of Blue, but only when I was alone. It was that painful that it had to be that way, it was for no one else's eyes.

I would think of him and then ask God for His strength, and He continued to give it. I appreciated everything and anything, all that was before me, and I understood whatever was ahead of me, It didn't matter the level of difficulty, I would do it for my son. I knew at a moment's notice I could let the scared and lost feelings overpower me. I made a pact there and then with myself that whenever I felt that seeping into my mind, I would remind myself with God and my son by my side I could conquer anything, and I would find my way little by little if it was the last thing I did!

I also made a deal with myself that I would be shown the path by whatever came my way, if I took the care to just believe and let things guide me. Whether it was something someone said, something I read or something I saw, I would try my best to not be fast and just truly live in the present for as long as I could. That way, all these little clues would not be missed and would not be affected by the speed of normal day to day life as it is nowadays. It can be done; if I did it anyone can do it. I did have moments where I panicked and thought that I needed to think ahead, i.e. like tomorrow or next week, but I would collect myself and make it stop. It's like breaking a lifelong habit, but it's doable. I would just get back in the saddle and remind myself the later and tomorrow would take care of itself, the yesterday's where gone, and my worrying was just that – worrying.

I had to go to Dryden Road Health Clinic for an appointment with a psychiatrist, a Dr Sutar. I got dressed as nicely as I was capable of. I had arranged to meet my friends Clare and Glenis afterwards for lunch. Jeans, white shirt, sandals and some slap, yeah that would do. Robert took me and we agreed he would wait in the waiting room rather than come in with me. My CPN nurse Lisa, who had rung me earlier in the week to introduce herself and to tell me about the appointment, came out to the waiting area. She shook mine and Robert's hands and then took me in.

Dr Sutar was sitting behind a desk in the lovely bright space, open windows all around the room. He was very handsome I thought, although I would have rather stuck with the same consultant thanks very much. He stood when I entered and shook my hand too. He asked how I was doing at home, to which I said fine, then a whole load of simple, general, day to day questions. I told him I was meeting friends after which he was pleased about. He said that he wasn't really into western medicine and said he believed in a more holistic approach. I asked him what he meant by this, to which he said like me meeting other parents that have lost children and talking with them or helping each other when needed and that was pretty much that. Then my CPN asked if we could arrange visits for her to come to my home to see me and do a little bit of paperwork. Off Dr Sutar trotted, saying in passing it was nice to meet me. I said the same back. I gave Lisa a few other details

INTO THE BLUE

and then we arranged for her to come out the next week to my house. All done.

Robert dropped me off on Low Fell, where I was meeting them in the beer garden of The Bank, which is really pretty. I was going for a Coke when I went to the bar but ended up getting a cocktail. They were sitting in a lovely spot, the sunshine splitting the pavements, it was glorious.

I loved the Tranwell, but I must admit this freedom was nice. I told them about my appointment and asked them if they thought it was as short and sweet as I did. They have forty years' experience each at the hospital. They agreed that they thought it was brief, but ITU is their speciality, not mental health. We had another one in there and then went to a Turkish restaurant further along the Fell – food was lush – then home. It was a nice change.

When I had finished reading those books I started looking into mindfulness and clean eating and supplements. If I did the trio, surely that would be an ideal combo? The mindfulness I'll admit was difficult for me, I have a wandering mind normally never mind at that present time. I'll have a conversation with someone and then I will automatically change it to whatever pops up in my mind. What can I do? I'm stuck with it, people's reactions are like Marmite, they either love the randomness or hate it. I also, most of the time, just say what comes to mind, so it may not always be appropriate, but it's never mean or bad. You see, since I was young, I always thought I was just eccentric and because I love eccentricity in other people, I really didn't mind it, in fact I grew to love being like that. Also because of my interest in people and how they tick, I ask a lot of questions.

Other traits are that I've got my ways inside and outside of the house. In the house everything has its place, even a stack of books must be a certain way or a candle, everything really. Outside of the house – terrible. On a night out, worse when I was younger, I would get numerous buses back and forth to change my outfit, sometimes four, five times – it was exhausting. I don't know how I just never stopped going out. My friends and family just got used to all of the above, I think because however much they thought it was madness they never really understood it, nor did I. I just knew I would be repetitive until I felt comfortable enough and then I'd be calm. Those things did crack me up but how much control I had over it I do not know.

So, food shopping I went, organic everything, from veg, to fruit, then sourdough bread, grass-fed butter and meats, kombucha the fermented drink, and some natural yoghurt. It was like getting a large prescription I thought, tick, tick, tick, I'll be sorted from the inside out in no time. On a serious note, when I stuck to it religiously, I never felt better actually!

Magnesium glycinate, vitamin D, ashwagandha, GABA, collagen and MCT powder, I got it all and I took it all. If you had turned me upside down, I would have rattled, but I felt great. Who needs a shrink and a CPN when you have all this knowledge and information at your fingertips? After about a month I binned my antipsychotic meds – I was bloated like a balloon and only because I have insight into myself, I knew they were making me totally numb.

I continued to see my CPN but I never told her that of course, what was the point? She was canny. She used to have a cuppa with me and talk about the weather or what new eccentric thing she liked in my house – I do have a few to be fair – but I didn't understand how any of that was helping me! She must have realised or got the message somehow, maybe as well because I talked a lot about my GP, Dr Ward. So eventually she asked if I would like my care transferred over to him, to which I agreed without hesitation.

I now had a routine at home, and it was going swimmingly – equal parts of fresh air, walking albeit solitary, healthy eating, sunshine, supplements, reading, bathing, sleeping, I was doing ok. I got a text to make an appointment with Dr Ward, so I did exactly that. When I went to the surgery for my appointment it never even crossed my mind about the last time I was there and being taken away in a white van. "Claire Hall," Dr Ward called, summoning me in. I was beaming, I was pleased to see him, he was a comfort for me, that had never changed.

He obviously asked me how I was, then he apologised for requesting my section. I wouldn't hear of it, I told him, and I was being honest, the Tranwell had been exactly what I needed at the time, and it had helped me immensely, and he looked relieved. As usual I told him the lot. I informed him that I had binned my antipsychotic meds to which he let out a laugh. He asked why so I told him that as well. He wasn't fazed, he said he agreed in some ways, though he did say in all his career he had not seen someone as unwell as I had been that day in his office. Then he went on to say he thought I was much better, and he suggested we see each other regularly for now, so every two weeks it was. I was on cloud nine when I walked out of the surgery, everything was coming together I thought, I liked a plan, a good one that is.

I walked home. I had also walked to the doctor's as well, trying to get some of the weight off I had put on. I must remember to tell Dr Ward that the next time, I thought, I had been so wrapped up in the thought of being his patient again I had forgotten. Whenever I walked anywhere, I felt like I had one of those old-fashioned diving suits on, you know the ones that literally weigh you down to the bottom of the sea. I don't mean my weight, this was different. It was about six miles there and back. Before all this I could have done it in my sleep. It was like climbing Everest now, but I was determined as you can see.

There were other things that were just as hard as well, as if my grief wasn't enough! The housework, which in my OCD days just a few months ago was a doddle, it now was a monumental task. I hope I can describe on this page how difficult it was for me. I spent hours walking from room to room discussing in my mind what comes first and how or where do I start and the more I did that, the more tangled and confused the puzzle of the housework was in my brain. It was absolutely awful. I could remember it being a breeze not too long ago, so that was sending me over the edge! It just made things worse, if they could get any worse. Why was this happening in my mind?

So, I had a tab, my old favourite way to have a think, and the only course of action I could think of was the same way with reading and now walking – I would just do it over and over again until hopefully it would become easier for me. It was like it was all brand new, like starting from scratch, so therefore I would just have to start at the beginning and hope for the best.

INTO THE BLUE

I stood again in the kitchen mulling it over for I don't know how long, then I just got so sick of myself, like I sometimes do from time to time. I put the music on full blast and then just got cracking. After all, how much could I mess it up, if I dust first, or hoover first, or wash the floors first or make the beds first, or do the bathroom first... do you see into my mind now? So, giving myself a pep talk – "Now get a grip, how bad can it be?" – pull my big knickers up, deep breath, a bit of disco or Motown and away I go.

It was like asking me to sort out Einstein's quantum physics, that's the level of difficulty it was to my mind, but I just plugged away at it. What defo did help though was living in the present. If my feet just wanted to go out the door and walk, well that's exactly what I did. It was unbelievably freeing and uncomplicated. I wish we all could live like that forever, but it is becoming more and more impossible to do. This world is now made for consumerism making us more and more wrapped up in all the trappings that come with it, or should I say, that's what we are made to think, me included, all the telling or showing us how we could or should live a perfect social media-style life.

I had another conversation I wanted to have with God. I wanted His forgiveness for all the turns I took in my life that inevitably changed the direction of Blue's. Yes, you guessed it, back in the garden. I asked Him daily, I told Him I wanted His forgiveness and Blue's for things I chose or did that changed both our lives. I do believe there is always a fork in the road and that we always have a choice. I'm far from perfect and there are things now looking back that I would have done differently. He did at some point, during all the asking for His forgiveness, give it to me. It was nothing short of amazing and felt totally divine, the instant comfort it gave me. Don't get me wrong, it wasn't as easy as just wanting forgiveness and so therefore I received it, no it was nothing like that at all. I was with all my heart sorry for some of the choices I had made, I mean deeply sorry, and when I spoke with Him, I told Him everything and exactly why I wanted His and Blue's forgiveness. I never knew before, but I know now that when you are truly ready to receive, God does not deny you in your hour of need.

In the February of that horrific year before Blue's death, it had been Robert's sixtieth birthday and for his surprise present I had booked a trip to New York for the November of that year. He was totally elated and surprised when he came downstairs on that Valentine's Day, yes that's his birthday. I had decked all the living room out with red, white and blue streamers and his presents were all clues – a New York skyline wine glass, a Lonely Planet pocketbook of New York etc. It wasn't hard to guess, and then at the bottom of the box were the tickets.

Now that my life had been turned upside down, we had to make our minds up to go or to cancel. We discussed it while I was still on the bandwagon of positivity and doing, so obviously I said no we didn't need to cancel, we should go. Robert asked if I was sure, it was a good few months away, so I said I would ask Dr Ward and if he thought it was a good idea then that was that.

We did end up going and it was only then that I realised that I was just a shell of the person I was before. Gatwick Airport was horrific. When we had checked our bags in Robert settled himself down with a coffee and his newspaper, so I decided to have a browse around duty free, as we had quite a

INTO THE BLUE

few hours to kill before our flight. The first entrance I came to – there are a few, the place is huge – I walked straight into one of Blue's favourite aftershaves, Terre d'Hermès. I couldn't get my breath, so I hurriedly turned around and there in front of me were shelves upon shelves full of Lancaster tan maximiser, the very same one I had to bring back from all of my holidays for Blue. Well, I was in a spin, I didn't even think I'd make it back to where Robert was. I went up the escalator trying my best all the while to slow my breathing, in through my nose, out through my mouth, trying to count to five each way, all the things I tell my patients to do. By the time I got to Robert it must have been blatantly obvious that I was in trouble as he took one look at me and asked what had happened. And was I ok? The only thing I could say was no! To which he replied what could he do? I pointed to the open-air gin bar right next to us. It was all I could do. I couldn't see a doctor, I didn't have a pill, it was the only instant calmer I could think of.

I sat down and tried my level best to do all my breathing techniques as incognito as humanly possible while Robert went to the bar. He came back with a double gin in a fancy glass. I just knocked it back and nodded to instruct him to go and get another. This time he came back with two. I did the same with those and then eventually I could speak. I told him what had happened and the way I was feeling. He asked what could he do to help? To which I said there was really nothing that could be done, only a doctor could help me. He then asked did I think I could manage the flight to which I said there was probably only one way I could do it, and that was with copious amounts of alcohol.

So off he went to find an all-inclusive lounge, cause at this rate our holiday money would be spent at this fancy gin bar and also, he knew I could have done with a cigarette. He came back looking relieved to have found one nearby, so off we went. To the bar my legs took me, ordered my gin, like Churchill said "Gin and tonic has saved more Englishmen's lives and minds than all the doctors in the Empire", so here's to hope! Straight out onto the terrace with my G&T in hand more than heavily poured by the very nice bartender. I wondered if he had any idea that he had just prevented a nervous breakdown to end all nervous breakdowns!

I took a large gulp then lit a cigarette. I did ponder if I should light two simultaneously but stuck with one. Robert had found himself a comfy sofa that had a slight view of the terrace, probably so he could check to see if I was ok without it being glaringly obvious. I did that for hours, bar, drink, terrace, smoke, repeat. The poor bartender must have thought that I not only had hollow legs but a big problem too.

I could have drunk at that bar for a solid twenty-four hours and not even looked tipsy or felt any effect either. It had everything to do with the way I was feeling that the alcohol never touched the sides. I don't know how long it had been since I had had a drink and even then, a couple of those and I would have definitely been legless, they were five parts gin to one part tonic. When it was time, I boarded the plane and I proceeded to sleep all the way there. Bet Robert was relieved, it would have been like don't wake the sleeping baby.

The hotel was lovely, the holiday was nice, I think. To be honest I just followed Robert around walking miles upon miles to all the sights which I didn't mind, but honestly, I know I was there, but I have zero feelings or recollections about it. Almost like I was drugged during the whole process, just a body and a pair of legs marching around. JFK time, time for our departure, round two. The same feelings started happening, that inner panic, like a small volcano about to erupt, only instead of volcanic ash it would be everything that was occurring in my mind spilling out and I bet more than a white coat job over there.

Poor Robert asked the same question, was I ok, to which I gave the same reply as coming, off to the inclusive lounge it was. NO FRIGGIN TERRACE! I was beyond devastated but I tried to contain myself. Yeah, I had my pretendy tab but it's not the same. Slight bit of luck though, the bartender must have been the one at Gatwick's brother, yes, the heavy, heavy pouring twins. Well, this is what I had so I would have to make do and mend! This time my hollow legs must have somehow miraculously been made solid the six days I spent in New York. Second extra-large gin in and it was taking effect. I did think for a split second that I may be in trouble here, like when it's time to board and then I just moved that straight out of my mind. This was for medicinal purposes after all and would they like the other Claire to please stand up! Somehow, I didn't think so. Absolutely plastered but got on the plane, slept all the way back like the same baby Robert took over on the outbound flight. We got the car from the airport car park, drove home and I could now say I had been to New York, but I'm guessing if I went again, it would all be brand new to me!

In the coming weeks I would spend more and more time on my own. I would use any excuse to go upstairs and just lie there on the bed. My favourite one was I was going up to read, which I wasn't, but it sounded constructive. Something new was happening to me and it wasn't just the torture of coming to terms with Blue's death, this was different but for the life of me I had no idea what it was. A very wise man who I've known all my life told me this when my mam died, he said to give my dad time alone even if I felt I couldn't. I asked why and he said to give him time to sit with his grief. It was another important chat that I remembered when I needed to. You see, if you don't sit with grief and try to run from it, there isn't a place in the land to hide from it and you can never ever outrun it, it will always, always catch up with you! I was sitting with it, but I knew there had been a shift somehow.

I think I was looking up grief and grieving on my phone – another one of my habits, I need to be as informed as possible, even if it's something I wish I had never found out. I came across an article a man had written about his own grief after losing his child and he talked about grieving oneself. I had never heard of it. He said he grieved his old self, the person he was before his bereavement. That was it! That's what I was feeling, it all just fell into place. I knew that the old Claire was gone forever, and my mind knew it too. That part of me went with Blue, that part of my soul had gone just like he had, and it wasn't ever coming back. When you lose a child, because they are part of your very being, your genes, your make-up, it affects you deep inside your core and your soul. A great loss that cannot be filled by someone else or anything else. A lonely deep chasm in your heart and soul and if your mind cares to go there into that abyss for too long it can easily get lost in the depths of its despair. But if you are lucky enough to have taught your mind to be in and out, almost like a freediver, they know they have limited time before having to resurface, and eventually that is what I did. I freedived my way in and out of my thoughts and mind, just the precise amount of time, not overstaying my welcome in case I did not make it back. There is a downside to this technique though, it's called guilt, because I wasn't sitting long enough with my newfound friend grief, albeit he had horns and like the little devil he was he would tap my shoulder, poke at me and nudge me all the time to remind me of this. That guilt of turning the grief off and on was hard to live with for a long while, but somehow my mind overrode it. Ultimately, I knew what I was doing was right. The new me, the new Claire, well that's all I had to work with, so I knew I had no other option but to get to know her and hopefully in time learn to love her again.

I went to see Dr Ward, and this time I told him about the issues I had been having climbing Everest! Ha! I mean walking, housework, any kind of activity. The heaviness I had all the time, like I said prior it was like having an old-fashioned diving suit on, or piggybacking another one of me every time I walked or did anything physical. I still walked down to his surgery by the way, and everywhere else for that matter, it's just in my DNA. He informed me that what I had was depression. I argued that no it wasn't, it was a real physical feeling. He reaffirmed, "No, Claire, it's depression." He went on to explain that severe depression can be real physical feelings like I was experiencing. I wouldn't have it, I argued again that I wasn't depressed, I was grieving, how could it be depression? I knew my son wasn't coming back. Looking back, he was right of course, but at the time I didn't want to grieve and have depression at the same time. I don't think I wanted two hits either, one was more than enough. So off I trotted, and I can remember thinking 'He's bloody losing his mind now, that's it, I'm defo up shit creek without a paddle.'

Never one to lose all hope though, I soldiered on and it wasn't too long before I needed to see him again. I'll have to tell you about this tale from the start!

It was a nice dry day and Robert had started jet washing outside the front of our house unbeknownst to me when I had popped round my sister's for a cup of tea. When I came home, I noticed that the ground was wet and I had flip flops on, and that's when the mania kicked in! How was I going to get to my front door? How on earth could I do it without getting my feet wet? I tried to think but my mind was unable to calm, I was distraught with panic. I hopped, skipped and jumped to my front door. God knows what I looked like. That didn't even enter my mind, I had only one thought and that was doing it with the least amount of damage as humanly possible. Then the next task, like going from one level to the next on a computer game, I was standing on the threshold of my doorway now but how could I step onto my doormat, I then thought. I could feel the splashes of water on my feet, and they were driving me insane. I took my flip flops off thinking that would give me some relief, but it never came. My next plan, looking up at stairs, which were straight to my left from where I stood, like they were a colossal sight, was to get up them somehow, and to be able to get to the bathroom. Yes, that was it! If I got my feet in the bath and was able to clean them, that would fix this problem!

So same game plan as before, I hopped, skipped and jumped with my bare feet up the stairs, much to my dismay

INTO THE BLUE

I should add. Then into the bathroom, into the bath my feet went, plug down, water on, bubble bath in, phew. I scrubbed them as much as I could, all for the few drops of water that had started all this. Towel dried them one by one while carefully stepping out of the bath. To my shock horror I still felt the same, I felt they were unclean and now how was I going to get from the bathroom to the bedroom?

Giant leaps, that's how I would do this final hurdle. So it was, four in total, then I dived onto the bed like my life depended on it. I felt like I was sitting on a boat in shark-infested waters, but I was safe for now, my feet were off the floor. I don't know how long I sat there too terrified to move. Eventually Robert came up and all the before was explained in a frantic fashion. Hence a phone call was made to my GP's surgery, Dr Ward would see me promptly!

I wanted Bertie to come with us, no idea why, in a roundabout way I relayed it, Robert just did as I stated. I say that because I had lost the use of verbs, so I spoke in a deconstructed sentence, awful I know. Bertie in his bed in the back seat, myself in the front with fully enclosed shoes on. Worrying on a level that was bordering on insanity, I knew my speech was a big red flag and my irritability was evidently visible. In front of Dr Ward, I sat trying my very best to explain what had happened with only the use of nouns. I somehow asked, "What is happening to me?" more or less, with a slight use of charades. This is exactly why I said before how brilliant a doctor he is, as he not only deciphered my words – you couldn't call it a conversation – he also told me what was happening. Which was when someone is highly stressed, they revert back to using only their frontal cortex, which is why I could not use any descriptives. He said when we were cavemen and women, we only had a frontal cortex, that brains were not fully developed at that point and that's what we go back to. He issued me propranolol and said I would be seen straight away if this did not pass or should it get any worse.

So, I got back in the car, leaving my club behind, only brandishing my script! Robert went into the pharmacy, came back and asked once again what he could do for me. I just said "Drive." I popped two propranolol, put the heater on the seat and looked out the window. I eventually felt slightly calmer when we were nearing home, bearing in mind we drove to Scotland and back! Yes, I live in the north-east of England, not far from the Angel of the North. He drove me, no questions asked, me looking out the window speechless the whole time to Scotland and back. I hope Robert doesn't read this book, I'll owe him some favours, I think.

After about a year, roughly, I went back to work. It was terrible. Covid had hit, masks, gowns etc, my lovely ITU unrecognisable, it had been sectioned up and our Rehab office moved to the bowels of the hospital. We had another ward designated for the non-Covid ITU patients. It was the worst possible way to try and get integrated back to work. Good job I've got nice colleagues, who in the main I've worked with from day dot, not to mention my lovely boss Susie and my wing woman Sonia, who I've also worked with from day one too. I honestly don't know what I would have done without them. The same course of action as before was applied, I didn't have a lot of options, I just had to crack on with it. Someday, maybe? I would feel like I had prior about work, loving my job and

INTO THE BLUE

the patients. My hopes were definitely a long stretch, of this I knew!

Chapter nine
Me, bipolar and Irene

Well, back onto the Bipolar, yeah, my version, but a real account of someone living with Bipolar. My next big episode was about a year later. My excellent boss, Susie, was going to do a secondment as matron for the winter pressure ward and a band six was going to come from ITU into Susie's job as a secondment. Well, I don't like change, I never have. Susie tried her level best to tell us in the most subtle way possible. Of course I wanted her to do whatever she wanted, even though I thought it was like sending a lamb to the slaughter. If you have worked in a hospital setting you know what I mean. She informed me that there were to be no new changes happening in our Rehab while she was away, there was no need. If I do say so myself, the Rehab works like a dream, we all had it down pat.

I was away on holiday at a fisherman's cottage in Scotland we had booked for a week, with Bertie of course, when the changeover happened. It's that beautiful where we go that this was about our third time there. It's in the picturesque harbour of Portsoy. On the fourth day I received a text to say that changes had already occurred at work, my texts back as you can imagine were unrepeatable . On top of that I couldn't ignore the fact anymore that Bertie had dementia. He wouldn't walk, he went to his bowls and forgot why he was there, it was awful. We had bought a doggy buggy to take with us so we could still do all our walks. It all started there really, and that mania lasted about three months.

INTO THE BLUE

When I got home, I still had a few days off and as soon as Robert went to work the next day, I knew exactly what I was going to get up to. I was getting ready when Val rang. I told her of my intentions, so she came to my house. I told her I was going up to work and gonna tell my new boss what I thought of her changes and exactly what she could do with them. Val tried her best to deter me, but it was falling on deaf ears. I felt so betrayed and insulted that only saying my bit would make me feel less disturbed.

As I was going out the door to walk up to work Robert was coming in. No conception of time had started, I had no idea I had spent half the day driving myself nuts about it all. He couldn't talk me out of either, so off I marched up to the hospital.

I would go straight to the office and if my new boss wasn't there then I would get her on Vocera, a hands-free device that you can call or message someone on. As I entered the office she was sitting there – well, that solved that problem, I thought. As soon as I went in she patted the book and asked if I had come to talk about that. Well, I had to collect myself. How she knew any of this was beyond me. Looking back she had obviously had the heads-up, that did piss me off. So, I sat down at my desk, and she was sat at Susie's desk. Here I go, I thought. I reaffirmed that I was told that no changes were to be made in the Rehab, as one, it didn't need any, two, we were supposed to be a team, making decisions together, three, this was just a six-month secondment, so why? All the while she scooted her chair over, closer and closer to me every time she spoke. I got all the spiel about why and how it was just a minor change, that it really didn't affect us etc, etc. I didn't believe a word, nor did

I think now anything I had to say on the matter would make a difference, it was set in stone cause after all a change, no matter how stupid it is, warrants people's promotions, banding and wages. I was long over all that about the NHS!

At this point I realised she was going to go on and on at me until I broke, insisting that I would change my mind and love it all, while I knew I was going to lose it big time. I sat now with my head in my hands on my desk, looking the whole time at the wall in front of me, while she still had not came up for air. Bearing in mind she is a senior nurse and I looked like Jack Nicholson in *The Shining* at this point, you would think she knew just by looking at me I wasn't well. But oh no, instead she kept patting her red book, like she was Eamonn Andrews, and this was *This is Your Life*! She had now stepped into the realm of not being able to see the wood for the trees on a grand scale. I'm not sure how long this went on, but I would guess around forty minutes to an hour.

Eventually I couldn't take it anymore and I lost my shit. Yes, I raised my voice, yes, I swore, I was like a caged animal in that office. Her voice was just a noise, I was sweating profusely, my face was on fire, and I screamed for her to look at me and asked how she could not see that I was not well, it all just spewed out. I did say, however, I still stood by what I said about changes and the stupid book. It was all pointless as she wasn't even listening to me. So, hell-bent she was, she never even realised what was happening to me, too busy with her barrage of speeches firing at me like bullets.

She backed her wheely chair away from me and pressed her Vocera. I shouted "Who are you calling?" She shouted back "Tracy." Tracy was my lovely boss and friend from the shop floor. I shouted back "Ok." She asked Tracy if she would come down, I heard Tracy saying yeah that wasn't a problem, but she would have to come and get her as she didn't know where the office was. As she walked out the door looking visibly shaken, I said, "Get her but I don't want you to come back" to which she said "Ok."

Tracy arrived. I was in the same position with my head in my hands at my desk. She however took one look at me and said emphatically, "Claire, you don't look well. I don't know what's happened but I'm worried." Thank the Lord, someone who understood me and moreover trusted my judgement, not once thinking it was impaired because of my predicament. I told her what had happened and that a five-year-old would have known to shut up earlier. She said this could have been sorted when I was better. But oh no, that never happened.

Tracy said that yes it was evident that I wasn't well and that it shouldn't have gone down the way it did, but she was more concerned about me, my wellbeing. She laughed when I said I looked like Jack Nicholson. I even had the scary hair. I have a tendency when I'm stressed to put my fingers through it and because it's wavy it stands up on end. She told me to go home and not worry about work and get better. That was me off for the foreseeable.

Much later when I was back at work, Susie had thankfully come back. Winter pressure was not what she thought it was going to be, least said soonest mended about that. The nurse that had come into Susie's role, who I had the words with, came and spoke to me and we cleared the air. Obviously when it had occurred it warranted another trip to see Dr Ward. When I told him what had happened, he asked "Did you swear,

Claire?" Don't know why he said that, I had always been as good as gold in his office, to which I replied, "Yes." He shook his head, but then I said, "So did she." He then said, "Aw, that's ok then," sicknote given.

A couple of weeks after that incident at work something really bad happened and just when I thought my mania couldn't get any worse, it did, because of what happened. I'm sorry, it's not my story to tell.

I had to go to town, Newcastle, to get some bits and go to my hair appointment. You see, it's not that I'm not capable, in fact I'm more than capable, as Dr Ward said I'm what you call high functioning, it's just the amount of trouble I can get into is no one's business. I'm not very appropriate and I'm also very excitable, which may sound quite innocent, but excitable and shops do not go together, trust me.

Well, I thought, I'll get there in good time, as time management, or any idea of it actually is not something I possess when I'm like that. I had a list on my notes on my phone, what could go wrong? I ticked a few of them off, I even called into my favourite shop, Fenwick's, to grab a couple of funky baubles while I was there. It was all going quite swimmingly, in fact triple checking the clock I had time to kill, so the first thing I saw was Costa, that would do.

I sat myself down at a table at the back with my large black coffee, like I needed the caffeine! I noticed a young guy sitting working on his laptop facing me a few tables up and I thought, aw I bet he's the manager working out the roster or something. Then three women came in and sat at the table opposite me. At some point the one that was sitting looking in the same direction as me spoke to the guy. I didn't hear what she said, but as soon as I heard his voice that was it, I was chiming in if they liked it or not. I said, "That's a Deep South accent if I've ever heard one!" "Yeah, it is," he drawled in a friendly voice. They didn't get a look in after that, so I asked him if he liked *Gone With the Wind*, to which he said it was his favourite film of all time. I told him it was mine and my mam's too. I then went on to tell him I had watched it hundreds of times. Considering it's an epic and it's nearly four hours long, that's saying something. He looked pleasantly surprised. I told him that I thought Vivien Leigh, who plays Scarlett O'Hara, was the most beautiful actress there ever was and that she and Clark Gable, Rhett Butler, made a stunning couple. His enthusiasm was now taking a hold too.

We chatted for a while longer, then I thought I should maybe get a wriggle on, so I gathered my things. As I was passing his table, I told him it was lovely speaking to him, then I noticed a book by his laptop. It was about Dolly Parton. Well, then I knew he was truly Heaven-sent, and I was supposed to meet him! Instantly I said exactly that, I told him I loved Dolly as well, I asked him was that why he was reading it. He went on to say that no, well yeah he loved her, but he was actually doing his PhD about her. I asked was that why he was in here and it turned out he was a lecturer at Newcastle Poly. I said, "I'm going to Waterstones now, I'll have a look for it," and before I left, he asked me if I wanted to see the tattoo on his arm of Rhett Butler and Scarlett O'Hara. I was over the moon, of course I did. It was stunning, it was done in black ink, I thought it was perfect, it must have cost him a small fortune. He said he had got it done in London. Made up with my meeting, off I went to the book shop.

Looked high and low but couldn't find it so I decided to go to the till and ask the lady to check. As I neared the front of the queue I noticed the display of books behind the counter. They were all the same, but the illustration was so stunning on the front of the book, all in black and gold. She checked for the Dolly Parton book, but sadly she said they had sold out but could order me one in if I wanted. I then asked her what the book behind her on the display was about. She said, "Aw, that's a children's book," I replied that that did not matter, and asked her what age was it? She said, "Age twelve." I said, "Ok, I'll just have that."

Leaving with my new purchase I decided to pop back into Costa before going to my hair appointment. He was still sat there, marvellous! I told him that they didn't have Dolly, but I did make a purchase and proceeded to parade my new book in front of him, *Julia and the Shark*. He then said, "I will look on the internet for you," and he found the Dolly book on Amazon for me. I thanked him and said once again it was lovely meeting him and off I went.

On time I think, I had made it safe and sound to the hairdressers. Did my usual and grabbed a few magazines to sit down with – well, I could look at the pictures I suppose, at a push read a sentence maybe, but no more than that. When I'm manic I couldn't read to save my life, it would be virtually impossible for me to read any more than a headline or a handful of sentences.

The girl who brought me a cup of tea saw Kanye West and Kim Kardashian on the front cover and asked me what I thought of them as a couple. I told her that everything Kim liked about him she would end up loathing, but he would make

INTO THE BLUE

it difficult for her and he probably would never get over their split. I added that she would have another Kanye in her eldest anyway. I said he would totally lose his way, and she just looked at me like I was nuts.

In the coming weeks at home, I either ran around the house or outside, not achieving anything, but in my head I was. In between no sitting whatsoever, only a small rest was had when it was bedtime, and that was only that I had to otherwise it would have driven Robert crazy and caused him any amount of worry. Night after night lying there with my mind thinking of everything and nothing at the same time, waiting for daylight to come so I could have permission to get up.

One particular morning it started snowing. I didn't know how fast to get up, quick wash, clothes on. Found my snow boots under the stairs, then proceeded to go upstairs to inform Robert that I was going out in the snow so to keep an eye on Bertie. We were taking turns with him by then as his dementia had gotten much worse. I decided that when I walked out the door, I would play Blue's Spotify list without skipping any songs, so they would be meant to be! Ironically, I started a playlist for him while I was in the Tranwell, the psychiatric unit, titled *Happiness Blue*. What was happy about him dying, I don't know! I'll never ever change the title or anything on it ever, I currently have over five hundred songs on it. It's totally eclectic, but whenever I hear a good tune in the charts, I'll add it – if I think he would have loved it, that is.

Aw, out in the snow, I can remember thinking God is so wondrous and powerful being able to send all this mesmerising snow to us. I've always loved the snow, I just think it's so magical and beautiful and that feeling has never changed since I was a child.

Stepped out my front door and immediately pressed play on *Happiness Blue*. The first song that came on – I had no idea as I just pressed play from where I had left off and never looked – was Roy Orbison's 'Blue Bayou'!!! Well, this walk was planned by my Maker, I thought. I've always loved that song, that will be why it's on the list. I do think the song is about Heaven, if you listen to it, he sings about seeing and meeting people again. He had immense tragedy in his life, much more so than mine or many other people for that matter.

While I was walking over the back of where I live, which is all just fields, in the cotton candy snow, the music like my very own orchestra for my ears, it was the nearest thing to Heaven I could think of. Then when Andrea Bocelli's 'Con Te Partirò' played, well my mind was truly sent floating over the snow-swept landscape. Every song had a meaning in it, albeit hidden, but my mind soaked each and every word in and my body felt the melody with each step I took. It was dark before I realised; I should make my way home.

Once home I had the same problem I always have when I'm manic: what to do in order to have the ability to sit down and to try and relax? I was stressing out, so I asked Robert for ways or ideas to help me sit down and watch TV. You see, all the ordinary day to day things, and I mean all of them, are a gigantic task for me. Like I told you earlier, I haven't got the ability to think of the before or after, so unless it's instant, using no thought process whatsoever, I'm incapable of being able to do it.

INTO THE BLUE

TV is overload at its finest, all the choices, all the different titles, all the genres, all the channels, I could go on and on. I just end up saving absolutely everything and anything on Netflix list and getting nowhere, no ability to make a choice. Ordinarily when I'm well I'll watch documentaries, the odd film and any reality TV, which helps me chill out. Not when I'm manic, oh no, it's all so fast and just noise to my brain. Robert, thank the Lord, had an *ah* moment and said, "What about old films? You know, the ones you watched as a child with your mam." At this point I would try anything to be able to sit down on the settee and watch something instead of walking around and around like a caged animal in the house. My mam and I would watch old movies all the time, I loved nothing more than to get settled next to her on the settee and get engrossed.

He found one, *The Bishop's Wife*, starring Cary Grant, it's a lovely film where he plays an angel. I sat as it started, fighting the urge to get up, and Robert sat with me for a little while. Hallelujah! It worked. I was not only not wanting to move but intrigued and a little relaxed as well. I don't know who was more pleased by the effect the old films had on me, myself or Robert.

At that point I had had quite a few manic episodes consecutively and I was so sick of them by now, not being able to rest, not being able to do normal things, but most of all what goes up, must come down! I now knew at this point that the downer, even after just a week of mania, can last up to twelve months. Twelve months of depression! My mania lasted months, this particular one was three months, so go figure.

At no point did the word Bipolar come out of anyone's mouth. My GP, Robert, family, friends, maybe they thought unless I mentioned it that they would leave it well alone. I must have buried it that deep inside my mind that it wasn't even in my vocabulary. Yes, I could say I can't sit down, or I need to walk, ultimately I knew I was different but left it at that, I didn't know any other. My mind was also so full there wasn't room left for anything else, let alone questioning what was wrong with me. I had grown to learn by this point whatever it was it would just have to run its course until my mind had had enough and I was exhausted and couldn't help but slow down. I continued with my new routine of walking in the day, avoiding people, places and old movies on a night, crossing my fingers and toes that it would stop.

The mania or being fast was becoming different to me now to how I had felt about it before. I think with Blue's death and the grief afterwards, the downer was like a massive black cloud looming towards me. I knew the storm was coming and I had no shelter whatsoever, no protection, no nothing!

When I look back to when I was younger, the manic episodes, which I now know to be precisely that, were much shorter and more rapid I think, if my memory serves me. So, the downs were for shorter periods of time, plus I'm a half glass half full so I could just shrug things off or at worst put a front on. The fact I was young made the speed a lot less obvious to me or anyone else. I think people just thought I was hyper, slightly scatty and eccentric.

But earlier in 2016, well before my diagnosis, my first big manic episode, or by medical standards an epic one, was after my mam died. I had six whole months of mania, that was non-stop mania by the way. I eventually got so sick of being fast, even though I had no idea why or what was happening to me, I asked Robert to see his son-in-law Patrick to ask if I could join the boot camp he went to. It was all run by guys who were ex-army. Patrick had become friends with one of them, and it was held at Leazes Park in Newcastle four nights of the week. I just naturally thought it was the only way after putting up with the first five months of it, to get rid. I had absolutely no idea what was going on with me except I was super-fast, unable to sit, unable to sleep, unable to relax, even unable to hold a conversation sometimes.

So yeah, I got signed up and did my first few weeks, going three times a week minimum. I was whopping the women and keeping up with the best of the men. I'm not athletic so it just shows you the power of the mind. Robert used to take me and wait in the car, but he would always come and chat with the guy who ran it afterwards, which just made me paranoid and pissed off. He later told me that the guy had said he had seen similar things with people in the army who had PTSD, but we all had no clue and Robert just thought it was still my grief.

It was probably my fourth week there and I really struggled this night, then the next day I was ill with my throat, and aches and pains all over my body. I remember blaming the water bottles we shared. Nearly two weeks later I was still ill. Robert was working away again, and I wouldn't let any of my family visit, my excuse being that I didn't want them to catch anything. Eventually my dad got sick of excuses and my brother came and took me to a Walk In, as it was a weekend. I saw a lovely young doctor. She gave me all sorts on my script, two different antibiotics and an antiseptic throat spray. My throat was horrendous, it was like swallowing glass, my tonsils had huge yellow spots on them, and I had no voice. I got a text message a week later to make an appointment with Dr Ward. I remember thinking, aw no, what's that about, a GP getting in touch with me.

I had first met Dr Ward when Robert had taken me days after my mam had died. I was super paranoid and quiet in his room at first. But then by the end of the appointment I lost the plot. It started with me showing him my toe, which I thought had an ingrown toenail and when he said it was ok, I could come back if it got any worse, I kicked off, clearly overly agitated by this point and not being able to hold it in a second longer. I stood up, pacing the floor and screaming, shouting I couldn't come back, not for a long time and that I was so sick of fucking doctors. Realistically I was, I had seen a lot of doctors and hospitals, excluding my job, while looking after my mam for seven years after her brain haemorrhage. He gave Robert some zopiclone for me and told him to say EXTRA to the receptionist if he needed an emergency appointment.

The next time I saw him was before I joined the boot camp, I thought he could help with how fast I was. I did play it down a lot, as I didn't want him to think I was a total nutter. I also omitted a few truths like the sixteen thousand pounds I'd spent in six minutes on the Mytheresa website and the continuing thoughts of grandeur I had, no he defo wasn't getting to know that stuff. He suggested I go to Talking Therapies, counselling if you will. I agreed, I thought it was bollocks but said yeah.

Day of the first therapy session, my friend Spires said she would take me and wait in the car outside for me which was nice of her. I was early so I just walked around and around the reception area reading the numerous posters on the walls. Time was ticking and I started getting pissed off at the fact that they were running late. I could literally hear the clock noise in my head, and I was pissed, thinking they were deliberately winding me up. Then this small middle-aged lady came out, she took me into a small room with a table and two chairs and asked me to sit down with her. She introduced herself – Vanessa was her name – and she asked me to introduce myself. All I remember after that was that I couldn't really hear her words anymore for my thoughts, like she was underwater and she was just a body on a chair opening her mouth.

Next thing I jumped up and started marching around the room talking about my childhood etc, etc, saying that may have to do with what was going on. In hindsight my brain was totally overloaded and stressed because I knew something was wrong, but I didn't know why and couldn't put all the pieces together, as well as the small fact I was deeply unwell. She shouted at me "Sit down," to which I replied, "I'm a pacer, I'm not going to harm you," to which she replied, "Ok, pace away," so I did.

Don't know what happened when I left, I would have thanked her though. Spires was still sitting in the car outside. I climbed in the car and she asked, "What happened, was everything ok?" I said, "Put your foot down and drive, it's a getaway white coat job," which made her laugh out loud.

A couple of hours later while I was walking Bertie, Vanessa rang my mobile. She asked if I remembered her from our meeting. Of course I did, I remembered thinking is she a nut job. Also, had I remembered that she said if she thought there was a need she would have to get in touch with my GP, to which I said yes, which was a lie but never mind. She then went on to say that she had done just that. Dr Ward was on a day off, so she spoke with the other partner of the practice. She also sent a detailed email to Dr Ward and made an appointment for me on the Monday. She said that she thought I was quite poorly and that it was above her position to continue to see me and would I please, please go to the appointment she had made. She also asked whereabouts was I to which I said, "Walking the dog," which I was. She then asked if I had had any feelings of self-harm, to which I genuinely and concretely said "No, never!" So, I'm thinking, she thinks I'm a fruit loop, well I'll show her. I said, "Vanessa, I'm not sure what you're trying to imply here but of course I'll go to the appointment and if my GP thinks whatever you're thinking then of course I'll do as he asks." She clearly didn't know me, I thought, as I would never not do what is asked of me from a doctor.

I did see him on Monday and he asked what I had done, so I told him and then he said, "I think you scared her." And that was the end of Talking Therapies for me.

So back to that appointment he had asked me to make after my boot camp throat episode, he said he had been waiting for this to happen. I couldn't figure out what he meant, after all it was the bloody shared water bottles. When I told him that he laughed and said gently, "Claire, it wasn't the water bottles, no one can be fast like that forever. Eventually you hit a brick wall." No truer statement was ever said! So that was my first big/long manic episode.

But getting back to this episode, I continued trying out my new routine of walking in the day and old films at night. It wasn't great but at least it was manageable and being able to sit down at the end of the day was a glorious wonder to me. Bertie in the meantime needed a decision to be made about him. He could no longer walk outside of the garden, and he went to his water and food bowls and forgot why or even what to do. He had to be carried up and down the stairs. It was no longer fair to prolong things.

We spoke and came to a joint decision that I would ring the vet's. I did however say to Robert that I did not want to carry Bertie to and from the car the morning of the vet's, so he agreed he would do that. Later, when I was better, when the conversation cropped up about Bertie, both Robert and Dr Ward both said unbeknownst to each other at separate times that losing Bertie would have had a significant effect on me. It obviously subconsciously had, even though I never shed a tear, I hadn't done that for anybody or anything since Blue. I was numb (or so I thought) to what was going on around me, maybe self-preservation, I don't know, but internally that seems to have been quite a different matter.

So, the morning came, Robert as promised carried Bertie to the car in his favourite blanket. When we arrived at the vet's car park Robert was inconsolable. Suddenly all I could smell was gas, didn't realise until a long time later that it was psychosomatic. The intensity was so great it was unbearable. Robert was incapable of anything at this point, but I didn't have time to wait, I needed to get out of the car away from the smell. Aw the fresh air was better, but still it lingered. I grabbed Bertie from the back of the car and told Robert to follow me in. They all knew and loved Bertie at the vet's, so that was one less hurdle.

I was ushered into one of the rooms, Robert followed, tears streaming down his face, then the very nice vet came in and told us gently in our own time she needed to take Bertie to put a cannula in his leg. I told her to just do it now. When she left the room, I asked Robert if he was just staying for me, or did he need to go? He confirmed what I thought, he said he wanted to stay for me but didn't think he could. I told him that was fine, for him to say goodbye when she brought him back then for him to go to the car and wait.

He did just that and when he left, I asked the vet what exactly was going to happen, what was the procedure as I had never done this before. She explained that I could sit with him for a while and then she would give him the drugs via his cannula, and it would be quick. I told her I didn't need more time and for her to just do it now. All the while the smell of gas never left. Just as she neared the cannula with a syringe, I shouted "Stop"! She looked at me, not knowing what to do. I apologised and said I wanted her to go ahead, but I wanted her to use her stethoscope as she was doing it, I just needed to know in my heart and head how quick it was, don't know why. She did as I asked, and his little body went limp in my arms. It wasn't much over a minute, she said. I thanked her, kissed him and walked out. The smell of gas had now gone, like it was never there.

As we had planned beforehand, we headed to the beach, although I had to tell him to pull over a couple of times in case he crashed the car with all the crying. I on the other hand just sat there in silence in the main for most of the drive. We parked up in a car park adjacent to a hotel with a restaurant attached at the beach front. I suggested we go inside first so he could have

INTO THE BLUE

a cuppa or something stronger – quite frankly I needed a stiff drink. Robert asked for a cappuccino, and I ordered a vodka, only to be told it was ten forty-five a.m. and the bar didn't open until eleven. That was ok, I'd wait.

'Starter's orders' I was out of the gate, up from the table and to the bar, as soon as Robert said it was eleven a.m. I wasn't upset like I said but I knew I had this inner turbulence that was making me feel unsteady, a horrible uneasy feeling. I would have rather had the tears any day of the week. When we finished our drinks, we walked along the promenade and then onto the beach front. Hadn't really thought this one through very well though, as the beach equals dog owners and dogs, people walking their dogs! Robert did not cope at all with it, whereas I stopped and stroked, petted and chatted to each and every one of them and their owners. So yeah, people could say I can compartmentalise but that's not what is really going on. All the bad things in me go to a deeper level where they take much longer to process, if they ever get fully processed at all.

In four years, I lost my mam, then Blue, then Bertie and then finally my dad. It was total wipeout. Even if I had wanted to, I couldn't have processed one before another one was gone. I idealised both my parents, Bertie was my little confidant and pal and Blue – well, I don't need to say really, he was my child. My mam was the matriarch, she was dry, funny, and still the strongest, bravest person I have ever known. My dad was a gentleman in every respect, he wore a vest until May was out, you would never see him without dress shirt and dress trousers on, even while gardening, and he was so wise and so polite. My mam would swear to make you laugh, my dad on the other hand, in all my life I never heard him swear, not once, you couldn't have got more polar opposites.

All of that is too unbearable even now to think of sometimes. To tell you the truth, only while writing this book have I first shed a tear for Bertie, that's how truly locked away my feelings for them are. I open the door with the key only now and again. It must be a safe space, normally when I'm by myself, mostly when I'm out walking or alone in the house, but sometimes it surprises me and seeps out. I will never throw the key away as I know the healing process is to let go of all the sadness, but because the pain is so monumental and huge I feel it can only be released slowly and in parts. Therefore I open the door for moments at a time and then close it again until I am able to do the process again.

The three months of mania had come to an end. Yes, I checked, I was still intact, done in, but still here, still going, albeit a crawl, now the party was over. About six months into my lull or down period I came across the book, the book I had bought back when I was manic, you know the children's book, the one with beautiful illustrations of black and gold on the cover – *Julia and the Shark*. I was well enough now to eventually read it.

All settled on my bed, late afternoon as I remember, I opened the first page. As you can imagine, it wasn't a long read. There is nothing on the front or back that informs you what the book is about. So hence I was reading it blind so to speak, not really knowing what to expect.

As I came to the end – I will not spoil it too much in case you may want to read it – I was in total shock, sitting on my bed in total clarity of my new realisation. Robert came into the room drying himself after his bath and when he looked at me, he knew something was up. He asked if I was ok. I said simply, "Robert, I have Bipolar."

I didn't understand how he looked like he did, as if this wasn't new information to him, he just asked how I had come to think or know that. I told him that's what the book was about, and you have no clue until the very last few pages. It's the mother who has Bipolar and I now knew I had it too. It took reading the book and maybe now the lights were on, and I was definitely home. Now I wasn't simply me anymore, I was me and Bipolar, my new twin, all jumbled up into one entity.

Robert then went on to tell me that that was why he had to have all those numerous conversations with my consultant Dr Sem at the Tranwell unit, so he could get all the information he needed to make a complete diagnosis. He asked him about me and my behaviour prior to all of this and his conclusion was that my diagnosis was Bipolar 1, Bipolar Mania. I asked him why no one had mentioned it and basically it came down to the fact that no one wanted to rock the boat. Well, now that boat was let loose and out at sea, 'a rough sea with enormous waves', without a captain on board, anchorless and little old me trying to steer it.

Now this was easily over a year and a half from my stint in the psychiatric hospital. So here I was with this new thing looming over me, or so I thought it was new. In the coming weeks I felt like an imposter walking around, not really me but also not someone else sort of thing. It was the oddest thing that's ever happened to me. I started doubting my own thought process, saying I've always been a 'what you see is what you get' sort of person and say it shit or bust, that was a full-on head fuck. I was reiterating conversations I had had with people, going over and over them with a fine-tooth comb in case I had been inappropriate or on the other hand not true to myself. The self-doubt, the anxiety, the thinking before I spoke, the people, places I avoided are no one's business during this time. I honestly thought, what's this? I've been around the bend nuts before, this is going to drive me there again!

I ended up at Dr Ward's again. I told him exactly what was happening and how I came to the realisation of my Bipolar. He is funny, clever but funny nonetheless, and he asked me to tell him the story of the book, so I did. The mother who had the Bipolar was a bit of an oddball and fast, very fast. He asked what I thought of the mother, and I told him straight up I really liked her, that made him laugh out loud! I just looked at him quizzically; he asked, I answered. He told me that I was experiencing a crisis of confidence and that it was fair enough really, considering. He then said I had had Bipolar all my life and until these horrible events I had managed quite well to be able to live alongside it all this time. I wanted to make doubly sure, so I asked him was I cracking up with all this self-doubt? It was affecting me even when I was alone. He repeated that I was still the person I had been all along and told me when that self-doubt occurred to just remind myself, I had had this all my life.

So, off I went home, Me, Myself and Irene, and when the mania came around again, I would be like Jim Carrey on acid, but you know we all have our issues. I can remember thinking how many people are walking around like me, probably millions, all the while ordinary people had no clue what was going through our minds but if they cared to stop and chat to us, they would probably be better off not knowing. I thought for a period that even I wouldn't let myself loose sometimes! But if Dr Ward thought I was good to go, who was I to argue?

Deep breath, pull my big knickers up and just wing it, that was as much of a plan as I could muster up then. Life would be – and was – like a minefield for a while, but I managed to tiptoe my way around the mines, not the tulips, until I got through it, without the use of any detection aids whatsoever. I felt like Lady Diana minus her protective vest and visor, more importantly though no the mine detector at hand! on a bad day, for I don't know how long, in my mind that is. I'm being honest, the daily battle was real. I could have left and returned home in an armoured vehicle, or a tank and I still wouldn't have felt safe.

Now two years on from that and five years since Blue died, yeah, I still have a couple of episodes of mania a year, which I'll just have to take on the chin, but thank God I've come to the realisation that it's something I will have to live with, and those doubts and lack of confidence have now shifted. Sometimes they do creep in, but I try to get rid of them as quickly as they come. I know now what can aid a manic episode or start it on its way. My close friends and family also now know the signs or signals and feel at ease to ask me if I'm ok or am I not well again. Robert now has an equilibrium about the episodes and me, which is such a relief I can't tell you as after I got rid of that awful self-doubt, he started overthinking everything, and I mean the slightest thing! Everything was a sign that I was heading south again. He has now stopped the panic, which was sending me over the edge for all the wrong reasons. I have to give him massive kudos, cause now he has got it right, he's owed a promotion to a shrink level that I never knew was possible. So well-done, Robert, I do love you x.

I also think I may as well take advantage of the other traits I have and maybe I just wouldn't be me without the Bipolar. I've decided to make it my companion not my foe. I always try to find silver linings in all the worst, horrific, horrendous situations I've been in. I think if you look closely, or more importantly if you want to look, you will find a silver lining too. My mission for the latter part of my life now that I'm fifty-one is to make my son proud and vindicate his death and pursue his aims until the day I'm with him again and my lovely mam and dad, as well as all my other loved ones in Heaven.

Last year I climbed three mountains, not in my mind these were the real articles. Ben Nevis, the highest mountain in Scotland, Snowdon, the highest mountain in Wales, and Helvellyn the third highest peak in England. I did have plans for this year 2024, but due to a back injury they have had to be shelved for now, but guess what my silver lining there is? That I got to write this book!

So, I dedicate this book to my beautiful son Blue and to all the people struggling out there like I did.

No matter how hard things get it is always, always better to pick yourself back up and keep trying, rather than to stay defeated or in a bad place. All the things I have mentioned in this book, i.e. from the coping with any kind of task, the housework, the spending, the beating depression, the self-doubt, the paranoia, the self-criticism, the unbearable heartache, the fixations, the feelings of grandeur, are not going to be there forever, yet sadly you have to go through them and live the journey in order to come out the other side. But I'm

INTO THE BLUE

living proof that the less you fight it and the more you help yourself during the whole process you will survive, and you will come out the other end the best possible version of yourself.

I realised quite early on that any move forward was a move forward, by which I mean go for that walk even though you feel you can't be bothered to even get out of bed. Make a goal to meet no matter how big or small, have a bath and wash your hair when even the thought of washing your face is too much. Your mind recognises these forward moves no matter how big or small and it rewards itself for them with a hit of dopamine, as a token of well-done you! I'm not joking, google it. I instantly knew it even when I was really poorly in the Tranwell, I really think that's how I avoided having to go to any more institutions. I've been once, it was great for me at the time, I'm by no means knocking it, but I don't want it to be my future.

You may get lost on your journey, as there are no road maps or Sat Navs, but I do believe there are signs. Granted you may have to look hard for them or get clues along the way, but they are there, make no mistake. The universe and Mother Nature want to help you, but you must walk with your feet and your mind to get to them. They're waiting, they are always waiting and will always be there for you.

Gut instinct, well that's always there too, but sometimes when you're feeling like shite, or at rock bottom, you may want to lie to it or ignore it, which you can, you're welcome to after all, it's your body, mind, life. But then the instinct that was told a lie to by your mind turns into the truth of the matter somehow. Don't do it, go with that first initial reaction and don't alter your course. Of course I've done the lot! The good, the bad and the ugly, but I soon got sick of the circles I was going around and around in. Unless you want to be stuck on a loop, take that leap of faith, trust your first judgement and keep going forward, you can't get lost going forward, that will only happen if you go off the beaten track or stay stagnant.

The journey of Life will continue to send us curve balls, some of our own making and some not, but we move forward with valour and faith and that will hold us all in good stead. We should never become, if we can help it, a prisoner of our own mind. I know some people cannot avoid doing so, which is so terrible, but for those of us who can, remember that thoughts are just that – thoughts, they can only control us if we allow them to. If we try our best to live from moment to moment until it becomes habitual, how wonderful life would be then, not troubled about what's occurred or by what hasn't even happened yet! Of course, for the rest of my life until my dying day I'm going to miss my beautiful son and feel the heartache that it has left me, but I also know that I want to serve him the best I can and make him proud with everything I do from here on in. I will make mistakes and I may fall, but I know that I will always pick myself up and dust myself down.

In a life that's more complicated than the days of old, but no harsher, just that bit more complicated, we have created more obstacles on our way to making what we thought would be a better life, a life of the future, ruled by things, materialistic and monetary. But we have what we have now so it's up to us what we do with it and how we want to live. The only time we no longer have a choice is when we meet our Maker, I believe. In the words and spirit of Helen Keller, "The best and most beautiful things in the world cannot be seen or touched, they must be felt with the heart." We all need love, hope and peace, it would be lovely to have them all at the same time and in equal measures, but that's not life. So, grab the moments when you can and bask in all their glory, don't allow them to be too fleeting if you can.

Believe me I've got a closet full of clothes, shoes, stuff, probably worth more than my house and it all means nothing. I've made more mistakes than I care to remember but now all I want is a simple, peaceful life and, when I can, be of good use here and there to others.

My wish to anyone who is reading this is that they can take something good from my story, whatever that may be, and to never give up the belief that life is there for the taking, all we need to do is to reach out and grab it with both hands. May you be valiant in your efforts and reap the rewards of your bravery.

Until we meet again my love, my free solo, my Chanson Bleue x

www.ingramcontent.com/pod-product-compliance
Ingram Content Group UK Ltd.
Pitfield, Milton Keynes, MK11 3LW, UK
UKHW040948240325
456642UK00001B/19